The Money Mindset

Master your Personal Finances

Vinay Mahajan

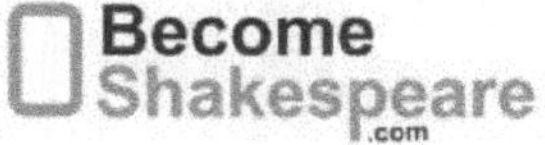

First published in 2019 by

BecomeShakespeare.com
Wordit Content Design & Editing Services Pvt Ltd
Newbridge Business Centre, C38/39,
Parinee Crescenzo Building, G Block,
Bandra Kurla Complex, Bandra East,
Mumbai 400 051, India
T: +91 8080226699

Copyright © 2019 Vinay Mahajan

ISBN 978-93-88930-39-0

Dedicated to

Men & Women

Who Dream

Author's Note

Time is our most precious resource. This resource is unique and it can work either in favour of you or against you, depending on how it is being utilised. In my interaction with clients, lack of time is the most common cause of not planning for major life milestones and essential life goals.

We are too busy to plan for ourselves and our routine work schedule seldom allows us to take care of our important life goals. Though priorities and liabilities are known, a busy life makes us helpless to plan on time. Time passes through faster than expected. One of our clients shared with us that he realised (surprised) about his daughter's readiness for marriage only when one of his relatives put across a marriage proposal to him. This is not uncommon and there is enough time to plan, only if it is done on time. I come across many such stories when I meet people and suggest a few essential things about financial planning, and the majority of them would agree that financial goals were known to them but they thought that there was enough time available to plan, as a result planning would always be postponed. Moreover, the majority of them would save enough keeping in mind major financial goals but still would not invest it appropriately.

I have also felt the satisfaction of sound financial planning when people shared that they have achieved a financial goal of securing admission for their kid into a college, which they had dreamt of. Also when they share that they can retire early from their regular work because of their planning, and when someone plans something big having experienced the power of financial planning. This simply comes from adequate assets for particular goals, or adequate provision for expected liabilities, or channelising savings through appropriate investment vehicles towards selected financial goals.

There are people who dream, and then plan and work towards achieving their dreams and these people are immensely inspiring. When a normal, salaried person dreams to send his daughter for medical education, plans for it, provides education to her and finally sees her as a medical doctor, that's the power of a dream. Financial planning surely works to achieve your dream. Only condition is that you should dream.

This book is an attempt to unleash the power of financial planning for those who dream and want to achieve financial freedom, an attempt to put forward a simple and workable approach to financial planning. I am sure this approach can be comprehended easily and will help all the readers who dream and want to achieve their dreams in implementing their plans. In achieving financial dreams, important tasks are planning and execution. The Financial Planning Year Book would help you in planning and execution, but it all begins with the dream.

It is said, "See dreams through the heart, it will always be achieved." You dream and dream more, rest this book would assist!

— Vinay Mahajan

Foreword

Finance is a very boring topic for many. We hardly discuss our financial planning pros and cons in detail with our friends and family. Most of the time people come to me and ask, I have some money with me to invest, tell me where I should invest? Have we ever experienced similar discussions with doctors? You go to a doctor and say you have fever and ask for a medicine. Will the doctor take out a pen and give a prescription immediately for fever? We all know that it never happens like that, a doctor will have to ask a number of questions to figure out why the fever came in the first place, what kind of allergic reactions we may have to certain medicines, and after thorough examination only will he prescribe medicine.

Why don't we ask ourselves such questions before we give ourselves any prescription when it comes to financial decisions? Why do we follow others blindly most of the time before analyzing what is really good for us? Is it because we feel these questions are not important?

We spend hours and hours of research before buying a mobile phone which is going to last just one or at best two years. Why don't we spend just a few hours trying to understand financial products before buying them?

My experience with investors tells me that for most of us it is very boring and complex. The jargon and technical terms used can drive away even a seasoned finance professional

The author of this book has done a wonderful job of converting a boring and complex subject into a fun and easy one. The acronyms used in the book will certainly help readers to remember core aspects of Financial Planning and decision making memorable, long lasting and more importantly implementable.

The calculations associated with Financial Planning process has also been written simply and readers should not face any difficulty in understanding the same.

If the approach suggested by the author is understood and adopted by investors, there is no doubt in my mind that the readers will be able to live a stress free life forever.

My best wishes for Vinay and the readers!

Sincerely

Kaushik Ramachandran
Founder and CEO
Dyota Solutions, imoneyplant.com
Bengaluru

Acknowledgement

Financial planning as a practice and subject is very close to me; I have had opportunities to explore this subject further by virtue of my profession. I acquired great learning and experienced true joy in working with professional colleagues, interacting with clients and participating in seminars on financial planning, however, I never thought of writing on this subject.

There are some moments in life that change the way you look at life itself. It was such an instance when my wife, Sheetal, suggested that I write a book on this and keep it simple, so a common man who needs financial planning the most, can fulfill his or her dreams. Writing this book was a thoroughly enjoyable and rewarding experience and I'm indebted to her for her support and advice.

I am greatly thankful to my employers, ICFAI, ICICI Prudential Life Insurance, Motilal Oswal Group, Anand Rathi Group and Bonanza Group, where I had an excellent professional environment to learn and excel. This book is a culmination of my experiences with fellow financial planning practitioners, clients & my colleagues. I owe a lot to financial services organizations for continuously putting efforts and resources in educating customers on financial planning.

I am greatly honoured with the association of Mr. Kaushik Ramachandran for his kind suggestions on how to improve this book, and for encouraging me to do further work in the field of financial planning, in order to empower a common man to dream and achieve his or her financial dreams. His foreword has added a new dimension to the whole experience of writing this book.

My sincere thanks to my friends and colleagues who critically reviewed the manuscript and shared valuable insights towards bringing out this book in its final shape.

I must sincerely appreciate the relentless efforts of the team at Wordit and BecomeShakespeare.com. My gratitude to my kids, Esha and Vedant, for their unrelenting enthusiasm that has made me work beyond my capabilities.

Last but not the least, I am grateful to my parents and Guruji who made all this happen!

Contents

1. Introduction

"Action expresses priorities"
- Mahatma Gandhi

Money makes a lot of difference. All of us would like to have more of it for a variety of reasons. Surely, we would like to put all our efforts to do much better when it comes to enhancing the quality of life, education of kids or similar important aspects of life. Indeed, money plays a vital role in all these and more. Though earning is the central stage of having money, how much you save is more important than how much you earn!

This book is not about how to save more but about discipline in savings, and the aim of the book is to create a second source of income from your own savings and more importantly, letting money work for you and finally achieving financial freedom and certainty which will eventually lead to a higher quality of life.

This book is for you, to let you achieve your financial dreams. The Personal Financial Planning Book is to help you to plan finances well in advance to fulfil your dreams. There are four golden rules of investment, which are commonly touched upon in a majority of financial education programs or investor camps.

These Four golden rules are: (and remember, **LIFE**)

1. **L**ong Term

2. **I**nvest Regularly

3. **F**ixed Financial Goals

4. **E**arly Start

There are immense benefits to following the "LIFE" rules, since every rule has considerable financial impact on the final outcome. Let's understand these rules one by one. For simplicity's sake, let's assume 10% p.a. return and assume NIL taxes. Assuming zero taxes is of course hypothetical, as it is said there are two things that are certain in life and one of them is taxes. Since people will be in different tax brackets, for the sake of ease of explanation, zero taxes have been assumed. Secondly, for comparing investment returns it is better to consider post-tax returns and for an individual, post-tax returns may also vary based on investment products. So, to keep it simple and clear, let's assume a post-tax return of 10% p.a. while explaining the LIFE rules.

Rule # 1: Long Term

The benefit of a long term is that a larger sum can be accumulated with a little investment.

Let's work through some numbers to get the feel of this rule. Assume you have an investment horizon of **20 years** and want to get ₹ 1 lac (This looks like a very, very long period but time flies very fast).

The amount needed today, with lump sum or one-time investment is ₹ 14,900

Or alternatively, amount needed per year, with systematic investment is ₹ 1750 (₹ 145 per month).

Now let's assume that instead of 20 years you have an investment horizon of **10 years** to get the same amount, i.e. ₹ 1 lac.

The amount needed today, lump sum or one-time investment is ₹ 38,600.

Or alternatively, amount needed per year, with systematic investment is ₹ 6275 (₹ 523 per month).

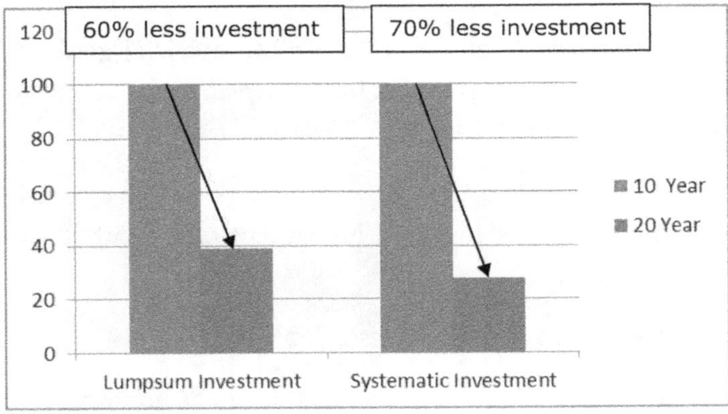

Illustration 1.1 Planning for a longer term helps in achieving goals with much lesser investments.

The benefit of a longer investment period is clearly visible in case of lump sum investment. For a 20-year investment horizon the amount needed is approximately 60% lesser compared to a 10-year investment horizon. Similarly, in case of systematic investment, for a 20-year investment horizon the amount needed is approximately 70% lesser compared to a 10-year investment horizon. It is quite evident that it will take a much lesser amount to adjust your savings if you are planning for a longer time period.

This is a very powerful concept and Rule # 1 allows you to plan:

a. For more financial goals or a bigger sum, since it takes lesser amount if the planning period is longer.

b. Better, because in certain investments, which are linked to equity market, risk reduces with time and there is enhanced probability of higher returns.

Rule # 2: Invest Regularly

Regular investment helps in achieving more financial goals simultaneously and with surprisingly lower investment for a given time period.

Assuming you have plans to achieve more financial goals, maybe even simultaneously, say you plan for 3 financial goals at one go and the amount needed is ₹ 1 lac after 20 years.

Amount needed per year per lac is ₹ 1750 (₹ 145 per month) for 3 goals and a yearly savings and investment of ₹ 5250 (₹ 435 per month) is needed.

Rule # 2 gives an edge to the investor's plan:

a. When done in a disciplined manner, this can facilitate regimented investment, i.e., every month or quarter or year, a pre-decided amount is invested towards pre-decided financial goals.

b. It will help them to dynamically adjust their financial plan for the better viz. by changing asset allocation or by stepping up investments according to changing income level.

Regular investment is further beneficial because as time progresses, income grows and investment becomes relatively small. In the above illustration, after say about 2-3 years, savings would become a regular habit and would hardly impact your budget.

Rule # 3: Fixed Financial Goals

Fixed financial goals means firmly locking in your personal financial objectives. Savings then will be directed towards appropriate investment, towards fulfilment of selected goals. This eventually adds to the certainty of achievement of the decided financial goals. Therefore, to plan properly, it is imperative to decide on financial goals and prioritise them. All actions would then revolve around fixed financial goals.

Rule # 3 helps considerably in:

a. Avoiding surprises and last minute rush to arrange for funds. Moreover, in any eventuality with adequate preparation, funds would be available to ensure that financial goals are achieved irrespective of changed circumstances.

b. Prioritising financial goals gives clarity of impact on financial aims and objectives in case there are changes in circumstances.

Rule # 4: Early Start

An early start gives money more time to grow and the powerful benefit of compounding comes to your side.

Continuing with the same example for a targeted sum of 1 lac at the end of 20 years, the amount needed to be saved and invested is ₹ 1750 per year or ₹ 145 per month. This is true if the investment has been given 20 years.

If investment is delayed by say 6 years, for the same ₹ 1 lac the amount needed to be saved and invested is ₹ 3575 per year or ₹ 300 per month.

It is evident that by starting late, more investment is needed (almost double in this illustration) since time to grow money is less and the benefit of compounding has not been fully enjoyed.

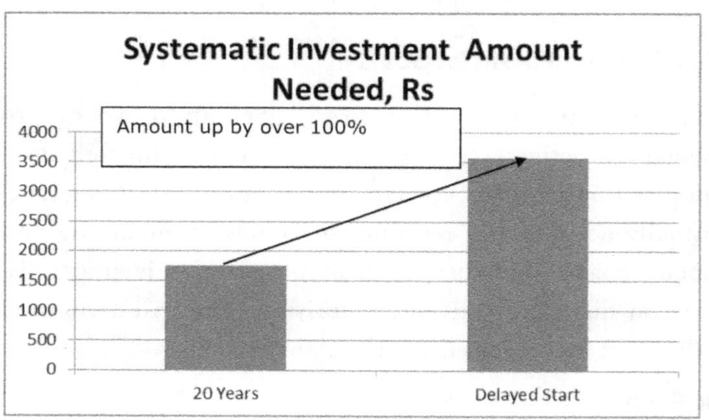

Illustration 1.2 A delay of 6 years would compel you to double the investment to achieve the same goal.

In this illustration, for ₹ 1 lac, regular investment in 20 years with ₹ 1750 per year is ₹ 35000 i.e. interest is ₹ 65000. Whereas, in case of regular investment in 16 years with ₹ 3575 per year is ₹ 50050 i.e. interest is ₹ 49950. Therefore, early start gives you the power of compounding, which is earning on earnings!

Major benefits of Rule # 4 are:

a. Lower investment is needed to be made for the targeted amount of money at the end of the investment tenure.

b. Easy to manage more financial goals with limited resources. Investments can be staggered after due prioritising of the financial goals.

LIFE rules can create magic if your meticulous planning has deep conviction and ardent devotion too. On following these **LIFE** rules financial goals will be achieved.

Just implement and see how miraculously **LIFE** works!

Essentially, the difference between dreams and reality is planning and execution. Financial dreams and their achievement too are no different. Financial planning and its execution can get your dreams fulfilled. Take the first step in this direction.

Let's begin…

2. What is Financial Planning: Know the Bigger Picture

"Plan your work for today and every day,
then work your plan"
- Norman Vincent Peale

Kaun Banega Crorepati? was a highly successful television show. You can also become a crore*pati*, in fact every one of us, with a little planning, can aim to become a crore*pati*. This is neither a scheme for any investment nor is it a lottery. With systematic planning you can add a few crores to your wealth.

Let's attempt to answer a few questions that can help in understanding the logic behind becoming a crore*pati*.

The first question: how much do you need to save every year to become a crore*pat*i at the end of 20 years from now, with a rate of return of 10% p.a.?

The correct answer is ₹ 180000 per year. The amount, as low as ₹ 15000 per month can get you 1 crore in 20 years.

Let's explore this a little more.

As we have seen earlier, for a financial goal where you need ₹ 10 lac in 20 years, you need to save ₹ 1500 per month. This logic can be extended to plan multiple goals or goals with varying amounts. Assume you plan for higher education for your kids in 20 years and assume that the amount needed is 30 lakhs (3 times of the target 10 lacs as above) then you need to invest ₹ 4500 a month (3 times of ₹ 1500 per month). Therefore, if planned early (remember **LIFE**, the golden rule) you can plan for a better education for your kids, and perhaps the targeted amount will not be a deterrent in securing a good education.

On the same lines you can plan for any of your financial goals. This is the power of financial planning—bigger goals can be achieved with ease, you need to just plan and plan well.

In the above illustrations, we have assumed a 20-year period and 10% return. In reality, time period can vary and returns too can vary. Return on your investments largely depends on asset allocation or portfolio of investment, i.e., where the investment is made. Asset allocation is an important decision, which is covered in some detail in this book. For example, with asset allocation, where average post-tax return could be 12% (instead of 10%) you can become a crore*pati* in 18 years instead of 20 years or for 20 years you need to invest ₹ 12000 a month instead of ₹ 15000 a month.

These are numbers, but money is also, finally, a number. So no need to be afraid; after all, it's mathematics of life. Start loving these numbers for a handsomely rewarding experience. Understanding these numbers and a few calculations helps you in making the most of your hard-earned money and will prepare you for achieving your financial goals comfortably.

The term "financial goals", which will be used extensively in this book, is also called "life goals". This is so because these goals are important goals and noticeable milestones in life. These goals could be buying a house, higher education for children & their marriage, planning for retirement, ensuring living standards for dependent family members, foreign travels, pursuing hobbies and so on. Indeed these goals are so important in one's life that they must be called "life goals". These goals come for sure in everyone's life and more importantly, one would like to maximise the availability of funds and secondly, achieve them at the stipulated time.

For example, a child who is getting ready for college education would need funds at the time of college admissions for various purposes. Surely, being able to afford a higher amount can help in exploring better options, including education abroad, if that turns out to be better in a chosen field of study. In a nutshell, "how much" and "when", both these questions are crucial. Financial planning is the answer to these questions. With proper planning you can ensure that you have the funds (answer to "how much") when (answer to "when") needed.

What about a child's marriage?

Well, life goals are important, and all goals should be on your agenda. Life is full of uncertainties and at the same time it is hard to predict the future, though there are certain actions that can bring in predictability and certainty to a greater extent.

To make the mathematics of financial planning more logical and easy to understand, follow this **"GOOD"** equation:

Goals Setting + Orderly Investing + Organised Review = Dreams Achieved

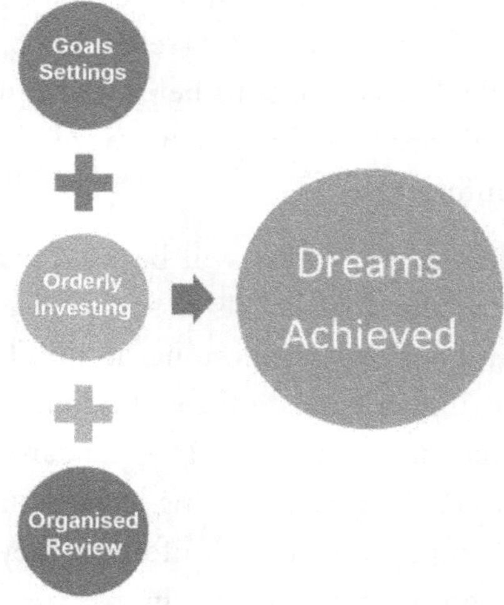

Illustration 2.1: GOOD Equation

To achieve desired financial goals, first and foremost, you need to clearly set financial goals, followed by initiating or realigning the investment plan towards set financial goals. However, that's not enough; both financial goals and investments need to be reviewed regularly to track the progress as per the plan. Once the financial plan is made, a review will not take more than 2 hours a month. With this little investment of time in the financial planning process, you can be ensured of a fulfilling future.

Let's go a little deeper to understand this "GOOD" equation with an example of a plan for a child's education.

Assume you need to provide for the child's education 20 years from now, for a post graduate education. Assume college fees, books, living & other related expenses, if admission is availed today, will cost ₹ 5 lac. How much do you need to provide for this goal? The amount, which needs to be arranged is not ₹ 5 lac. Why? This is the cost of education if admission is taken today. In this example, admission will take place 20 years from now. So we need to look at the cost, what it would be, 20 years from now.

Assuming inflation to be 6% p.a. (simplistic assumption for understanding, actual inflation may depend on the subject under consideration) then at the time of admission one needs to provide for a little over ₹ 16 lac. That's too high, but it is a fact that one needs to arrange for this much! Not to worry, though, there is a "GOOD" solution. You need to invest ₹ 2.4 lac lump sum today to provide for ₹ 16 lac (amount in today's cost terms) at the time of admission. This can be made further "GOOD" by regular investment of ₹ 28000 every year or ₹ 2350 every month. Isn't it really "GOOD"? It is!

These calculations are approximate and have been done assuming a rate of return at 10% p.a.. For such a long planning horizon, better returns on investment are possible with asset allocation. This can be further sweetened by making investment more tax efficient, and also by tax savings investment to enhance post-tax returns.

There could also be a combination of lump sum and regular investment. In this case, for example, it could be ₹ 1.2 lac lump sum investment today and a regular investment of ₹ 1175 per month, with or without tax efficient & tax savings investments. There could be similar and more combinations available which suit your cash flow as well as your risk profile.

What if regular savings mode is chosen and due to some unfortunate circumstances it got disturbed? This could happen due to several reasons viz. due to medical emergencies, finances may get derailed or in extremely unfortunate cases the breadwinner may expire. Protection is the solution in both these cases. With adequate medical & life protection in place, the goal would be achieved.

Continuing with the above example, as 20 years' time horizon is quite long, the chosen investment would require regular review due to several reasons. A better investment opportunity may come up, the chosen investment may undergo structural changes, underlying market and investments may under-perform or over-perform, government regulations may change etc., but 20 years is a good enough longer horizon to achieve financial goals for sure. Do remember that as the goal approaches, asset allocation needs to be changed towards cash-oriented investment to add to the certainty in fulfilling the goal in a "GOOD" way.

The review can be scheduled once a quarter, on important event dates like a budget date or any event which may potentially impact chosen investments.

Therefore "GOOD" i.e.

Goals Setting (Kids' education, in 20 years, for ₹ 5 lac) with

+

Orderly Investing (Planning for ₹ 16 lac, lump sum or regular investment or combination) combined with

+

Organised Review (Once in 3 months or on important events) will ensure

=

Dreams Achieved on time

Just imagine the joy and satisfaction of getting admission for your child in a dream college for a dream education, for which you have planned for all these years. Further imagine during the year how worry free you would be and the level of confidence you would be enjoying! Isn't it a beautiful dream? It is indeed! Just imagine more!

Adding to certainty is one of the key objectives of financial planning, bringing in confidence and a smile on your face are just by-products!

What is financial planning after all? It is a way to ensure financial security and achieve financial freedom. It focuses first on maximising savings by examining expenses and directing savings towards investment to achieve targeted financial goals.

It can be said that "financial planning is a process of analysing and setting up financial goals, prioritising them, estimating existing resources and drawing a detailed executable financial plan and completing the plan to achieve financial goals followed by regular review."

It is evident that financial planning is not a scheme or investment or even an end result ; it is a continuous process, a process which begins with preparing a financial plan and continues till financial plans are achieved.

Why is financial planning a continuous process? Why does it continue till financial goals are achieved? Well there could be several reasons, which are specific to an individual and a few of the instances can be outlined here.

To address the questions, "Why is financial planning a continuous process?", let's revisit GOOD LIFE. In order to keep **"GOOD"** **(G**oals Setting, **O**rderly Investing, **O**rganised Review, **D**reams Achieved) "LIFE" (**L**ong Term, **I**nvest Regularly, **F**ixed Financial Goals, **E**arly Start), the process needs to be continuous.

First and foremost is setting up the goals. And as you progress in life, more financial goals can be added and also with time goal priority may change. Goal priority may also change not because your priorities actually changed but because one of the top priority goals is well on track and you need to work on other goals.

For example, for parents, their child's education and marriage are two important goals. With priority tag, goal no.1 is education and goal no. 2 is marriage and they start working towards achieving these goals in the same order.

Goal Priority # 1 Education
Goal Priority # 2 Marriage

After a certain time period, it may so happen that goal no. 1, i.e., education is certain as per the plan and now priority shifts to marriage. Since funds needed for educational goal look sufficient, as time progresses career choice also becomes certain and what has been done so far for achieving this goal matches the requirement. Though goal continues, only priority shifts to number 2. Therefore, after a period of time it may so happen that,

Goal Priority # 1 Marriage
Goal Priority # 2 Education

There could also be the case that a new goal emerges, assuming that after certain years of education, the child demonstrates extraordinary talent in a certain field and you find that it would be great if the child does something of his/her own. So you plan for an entrepreneurial venture.

New priority emerges now, so it may so happen,

Goal Priority # 1 Education
Goal Priority # 2 Business Fund
Goal Priority # 3 Marriage

Let's go a little further. Once a financial goal is fixed we need to save and invest to achieve that financial goal. Choice of an investment or investment mix (also called asset allocation) depends on your risk profile, knowledge about investment avenues, availability of advice & transaction facilities, prevailing tax laws, size of investment and other similar factors including current level of income.

Changes in any of the underlying factors can change your ongoing financial planning and you need to change the plan accordingly. For instance, you have kept a fixed deposit in a bank at say 8% p.a. and you come to know that the debt scheme of a mutual fund offers better post-tax yield, say 9.5% p.a. Since this information or investment or opportunity was not available at the time of initiating investment for a particular financial goal, you may like to revisit your investments. This depends, of course, on your risk profile and your understanding of the inherent risks in the underlying of the investment instrument. What if the Finance Minister announces an investor-friendly scheme? Will you take advantage of that? You should!

Let's assume, while you have planned for your goals, and your savings are just sufficient to meet fixed financial goals, you get a good salary raise at your job or your business starts delivering more profit to you. Won't you like to go for a long vacation abroad with the family, maybe after 2 years or would you like to gift something precious to your parents, maybe after 1 year? A bigger car? A second home? A farm house? Or do something that was a long-suppressed hobby of yours! With higher income, now you would like to do it, wouldn't you? Think for a while, does a higher income level make you take a little more risk?

Changing circumstances, goal priorities, performance of investments and similar other factors are the reasons which keep financial planning a continuous process and "GOOD LIFE" a dynamic "LIFE".

There are certain terminologies used like risk, risk profile, asset allocation, investment products etc. that may not be understood now, but no need to worry as these are deliberately introduced here and elaborated in the subsequent pages.

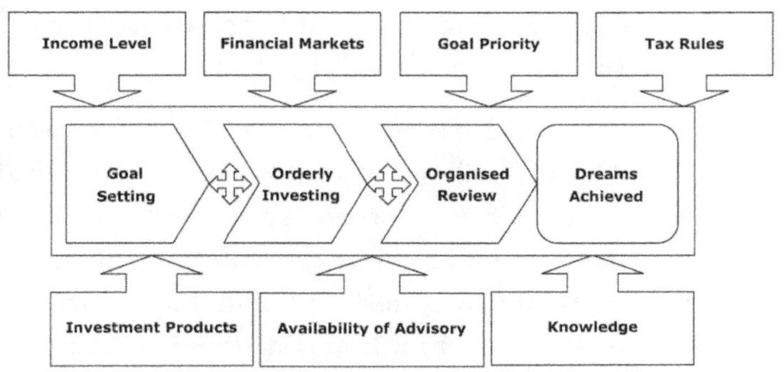

Illustration 2.2: Financial planning is a continuous process

There are two ways to look at financial planning. One is comprehensive financial planning, and another is goal-based independent financial planning. The former is the way to go, whereas the latter is a kind of intermediary stage, which should eventually lead to a comprehensive financial plan. Financial planning, per se, is a comprehensive process. Important elements of financial planning are provisioning for something unexpected by providing for contingency funds and providing for protection by way of adequate insurance e.g. medical insurance, property insurance, and life insurance etc.

Financial planning, as you will appreciate, can change the way you look at your financial dreams. Financial goals will be within your reach, much realistic and with measurable progress. You will be in complete command and dependent members will always be able to get what has been planned for them, at least financially.

To reinforce the importance of financial planning, let's look at why one should go for financial planning. The habit of saving is not new to us; in fact Indians are the biggest savers. On an average, we save 30% of our income (national average). Saving money for a rainy day has been a tradition, which we learn as a core value. Underlying fundamentals are undergoing tremendous changes and changing faster. This envisages that importance of financial planning will be much more as we progress further.

One evident change that can be appreciated is rising life expectancy, which has gone up and will go up further due to better medical facilities. Higher life expectancy for sure is good news but one needs to provide for funds to enjoy life with same or better living standards for a longer period. Moreover, medical facilities also come with a high cost and provisioning for medical exigencies is a must.

Another important aspect is changing lifestyle needs. Earlier, a home PC used to be a dream; nowadays, costly smartphones may become a necessity.

A few reasons make financial planning not only important but a must for everyone, simply because these factors have major financial implications and planning can provide for their implications, and absence of planning can disturb normal family life:

1. Access to information & advice
2. Availability of financial products
3. Ever changing lifestyle needs
4. Higher health care costs
5. Increasing life expectancy
6. Inflation
7. Regulatory changes
8. Nuclear family
9. Uncertainties with regard to income source
10. Volatile financial markets

Financial planning needs your commitment, not just your involvement, not only because it is for your own benefit but also for two other important reasons. One, there is cost involved in not planning and second, more benefits can be drawn if planning is done appropriately. In case of the former, what is the cost if you do not plan? Most visible cost is inflation, which is not in anyone's control.

Your financial goals will become dearer by every passing year and all the while you do not enjoy the benefit of financial planning. Secondly, with appropriate planning with the same investment, you can get more amount at maturity or for the same amount you may need to invest a lesser amount.

Let's understand this by an example. Assume you invest ₹ 5000 per month towards a financial goal 20 years from now and your chosen investment gives a return of 8% p.a. On an average, over a 20 years horizon, you get ₹ 27.5 lac. With a little effort or advice, assume you are able to invest where returns are 10% p.a., you will get in the same period for the same amount of investment, a return sum of ₹ 34.4 lac. The difference is approximately 7 lac. This is a whopping sum of money and if a little effort, understanding and study can get you this much more wealth, you should put all possible efforts to acquire wisdom! What if former return is pre-tax return and latter is post-tax return? The difference would be much higher!

It makes sense to put more efforts to increase knowledge about personal finances! It will simply make you richer! Indeed, as we said at the beginning, money makes a lot of difference, doesn't it?

Indeed it does!

3. Why Financial Planning is Important: Live Life King Size

"Think ahead. Don't let day-to-day operations drive out planning"

- Donald Rumsfeld

Saving for a rainy day is an old bedtime story, which still has huge relevance today. This story probably had a big impact on us and maybe, because of this we are traditionally good savers. Though saving is the first step and it's a good habit, however, saving alone is not sufficient. Though savings has its own importance, it has to be invested to earn a real rate of return. Further, if investments are directed towards a goal, savings will culminate in its ultimate goal.

Sometimes, it so happens that our pockets are empty and we tend to borrow from someone in the family, mostly from the mother, the only bank that lends when you need the most. Though we pay back to her the same or a higher amount without interest calculations, expectations are there that in case of a need in the future, she would rescue again. Such small borrowings are for a short period, a few days to a few months. Just imagine how someone would get financial help in the time of need if the time for which the funds are needed is fairly long (a few years), and the amount is too large (a few lacs)? Who would help? You! You alone could be of help to yourself!

Financial planning does that for you. The need for funds arises because there is asymmetry in income cycle and expense cycle during the lifetime.

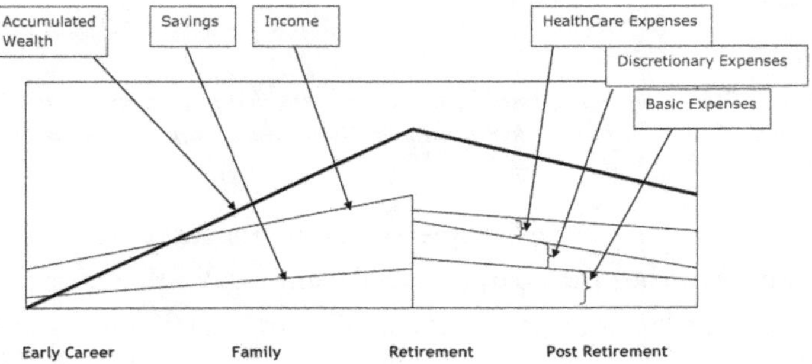

Illustration 3.1 Asymmetry in income and expense cycle envisages need for financial planning. During the retirement years it is visible that there is no income from work but expenses continue.

From the day you start earning until retirement (retirement does not mean end of working, it is an indicative time where an individual stops working to make a living, though working can continue as usual), income has a particular pattern but unfortunately income cycle is shorter. Income is mostly predictable, at the same time subject to the risk that income may get lower due to changes in employment or business conditions. On the other hand, the Expense cycle is an extended one, it continues till the end and please remember it continues even post life for dependent family members. Given a chance, one would like to spend more on things of his or her interest, and also uncertainties and exigencies make expenses unpredictable to a certain extent.

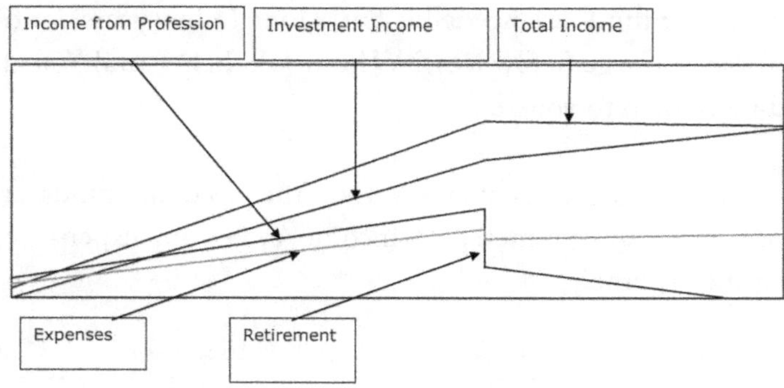

Illustration 3.2 Income – Expenses Cycle gives an idea that income from profession can lead to second source of income, which is income from investments to take care of future expenses

Therefore, income cycle is different from the expense cycle. This asymmetry can be bridged by financial planning. With understanding of income cycle and expenses cycle, planning for finances would be much more evolved and you would be able to provide for expenses by directing income to a targeted financial goal.

With financial planning you can plan for major life goals comfortably. Essential life goals like kids' education, their marriage, buying a home, retirement, to name a few must be planned as soon as you can. Financial planning has many benefits; one of them is helping you in creating your "DREAM WORLD". We'll see how!

In an individual's professional career there are two important forms of success- professional success and financial success. Financial planning directly helps in financial success and once financial success is in sight, it is more likely that the individual will also be professionally successful. Being financially successful also means getting sufficient funds in the future when needed, and planning can make it happen. This is done by understanding current expenses, expected funds requirements in the future and appropriate investment vehicle with necessary protection. Therefore, financial success does not only mean quantum of money one makes but the optimum utilization of the limited money that you have.

In financial planning, we talked about various financial goals. What are these goals? It is not just about owning a house, a holiday abroad, kids' education or their marriage, etc. In fact, it is about moving to a higher living standard from the present standard of living. Financial planning is therefore a conscious choice of an individual for the benefit of the self and his family members, which can result in two things, Financial Success and a continuously improving standard of living.

The benefits of financial planning are "**DREAM WORLD**"

D	**D**efined objectives	What is to be achieved and when to be achieved
R	**R**egimented approach to life goals	One goal is separate from others and planning ensures that planned goals are achieved with discipline
E	**E**ffective Protection	Adequate protection to goals from any exigencies
A	**A**ssured future	More certainty about financial security
M	**M**aximum benefits of investment opportunities and prevailing rules	Benefit from Tax rules, investment instruments and protection plan in your favour
W	**W**ider & Comprehensive Investment Plan	Longer term investment plans for all financial goals irrespective of the fact whether it was commenced today or not
O	**O**ptimised living standard	Better control on present and future resource to plan an enhanced living standard
R	**R**isk profile based investment	Investment plan suited to your risk appetite hence market movements will not worry you

L	**L**ife Stage Planning	Financial planning for your life stages
D	**D**esired update of credit score, loan worthiness	An up-to-date and sound financial record keeps your credentials high.

Financial Planning Score

It is sometimes difficult to objectively comprehend our preparedness to set financial goals. The following section helps in objectively quantifying how well you have planned your financial objectives. Just answer the question with confidence to see how far you have come up in essential financial goals.

Just write "YES" if you are sure about the question or write "NO" if you are not sure. Each question carries 20 marks.

I. Retirement Planning Score

Question No.	Question	Answer (**Yes or No**)
1	I know when I can retire	

Question No.	Question	Answer (**Yes or No**)
2	I know the corpus needed at the time of retirement	
3	I know the way to save and invest for retirement	
4	I will have the desired corpus to sustain me post-retirement	
5	I understand the impact of inflation on my retirement	

II. Wealth Creation Plan

Question No.	Question	Answer (**Yes or No**)
1	I know my net worth	
2	I know how money is being spent	
3	I know how much needs to be saved to achieve financial goals	
4	I know my risk profile	
5	I know the asset allocations of my investments	

III. Kids' Financial Planning (Education/Marriage/Other) Score

Question No.	Question	Answer (**Yes or No**)
1	I know the best way to save & invest for kids' education	
2	I know the time and amount needed for this financial goal in the future	

Question No.	Question	Answer (**Yes or No**)
3	I know how much needs to be saved today to achieve financial goals	
4	I have adequately protected financial goals	
5	I have asset allocation planning in place to ensure certainty	

IV. Protection Planning Score

Question No.	Question	Answer (**Yes or No**)
1	I know the relationship between financial liability and life insurance	
2	I know my total outstanding financial liability	
3	I know amount needed now to secure my family's future	
4	I am adequately covered under a scheme of medical insurance	
5	I am aware about my asset protection needs	

V. Life Goals Planning

Question No.	Question	Answer (**Yes or No**)
1	I have written my financial goals	
2	I know the impact of inflation on my financial goals and provided for it	

Question No.	Question	Answer (**Yes or No**)
3	I have prioritised my financial goals and started its execution	
4	I have retirement planning as one of the goals	
5	I review or will review goals once in every six months	

Score: Score 20 for each YES and 0 for Each NO

Financial Planning	**YES**	**NO**	**Score**
I. Retirement Planning Score			
II. Wealth Creation Plan			
III. Kids' Financial Planning (Education / Marriage / Other) Score			
IV. Protection Planning Score			
V. Life Goals Planning			
Total			
Average Score			

How to read the score: Since all the sections may not be applicable to you, therefore score of the relevant sections and average score is to be considered. For a particular section and for overall financial planning, average score to be read as under

Average Score	**Grade**	**What your score says about your financial planning preparedness**
80-100	A	Your financial planning is meeting your requirement at present, need to dynamically monitor financial plan

Average Score	Grade	What your score says about your financial planning preparedness
60-80	B	Considerable action has been done to begin with financial planning, need to move to a better score
40-60	C	Financial planning is in the initial stages and you are partly prepared, though a detailed planning needs to be initiated at the earliest
0-40	D	Financial planning needs to be given due consideration immediately

Your Financial Planning Grade is

Based on your Financial Planning Score, the task would be

1. To move to convert all "NO" to "YES" and thereby
2. Move to score perfect "100" and
3. Always maintain grade "A"

Life Stages

Having worked on your financial planning score, which gives an objective picture about your preparedness to financial planning, let's understand about life stages to take maximum benefit of financial planning process. Understanding life stages is not difficult, we see kids growing, going to school and then college, joining a profession, acquiring a family and so on. It is quite obvious. Comprehending requirements in these life stages is also not difficult. Only part which is tough is to begin planning and preparing for challenges which you may come across while passing through these stages. If prepared well, every stage would be very enjoyable and if not, implications can have undesirable imprints.

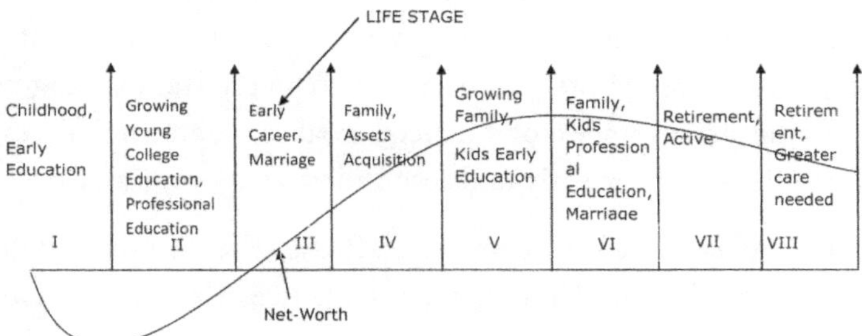

Illustration 3.3: Indicative life stages (Stage I to Stage VIII) from childhood stage to post retirement periods with indicated net worth movement with increase in time it starts with Negative figure since there is no income, grows, reaches at the peak and then declines in post-retirement period.

Financial planning prepares you ahead of the need, ready with funds at the time when needed. It keeps you close to reality and not too dependent on hope. With a well-strategised financial plan in place, you are prepared to take on the intricacies of life stages. These financial plans are simple to prepare, easy to understand, and easy to implement too. The only task is to begin, if you have not started yet.

Financial planning helps in taking better control of your finances, decision making becomes more regimented and the impact of a financial decision on decided financial goals is better visible. Impact of a financial transaction or changes are better interpreted as an impact on short-term or long-term life goals. For example, for short-term liquidity needs, instead of withdrawing from existing investments, availing a loan would be an alternative to consider. One would come across similar instances where it is better to fully understand the impact of a certain financial product before you actually begin transactions.

How to take maximum benefits of Financial Planning – RICHER

Financial Planning is a continuous process, more than that it is a habit. Since the financial goals span over a number of years, it is quite likely that underlying factors will undergo changes. These changes will impact the achievement of financial goals, therefore changes need to be understood correctly and responded to appropriately.

Changes in the underlying factors, if adverse, the response will be to save financial goals from the consequences. If changes are favourable, the response will be to take benefit of the changes. In both the cases, response will be needed and an apt response ensures maximum benefit of financial planning. A word of caution here, it is not about timing the market but about taking informed decisions keeping in view a particular financial goal and ensuring that it does not impact other financial goals.

Let's understand this with an example. There are two financial goals: the first is planning to accumulate down payment for availing the home loan in 2 years and the funds are invested in the debt fund of a Mutual Fund Scheme. The second one is retirement planning for 30 years, where at present investment is being made in a large cap diversified fund, with debt fund in the ratio of 70% equity 30% debt. Due to good earning season it is expected that equity market will do better in the coming years. Based on this information, you may decide to change the ratio from 70:30 to say, 80:20 i.e. 80% large cap diversified fund and 20% debt fund. Or in the same case, it is expected that interest rates will be falling in the near future based on economic scenario. With this information, you may decide to change the ratio from 70:30 to say 60:40 i.e. 60% large cap diversified fund and 40% debt fund. Once the economic scenario changes, again the ratio may can be revised to the original, taking into consideration how close the financial goal is. However, this information will not impact investment planning of the goal where you are accumulating down payment for availing a home loan, since it is too short a horizon to effect these changes.

In a nutshell, to maximise benefit of financial planning in a dynamic environment, you can plan to be **RICHER** too. RICHER is:

1. **R**egular review
2. **I**nformation
3. **C**urrent finances
4. **H**orizon
5. **E**valuate
6. **R**ealistic expectations

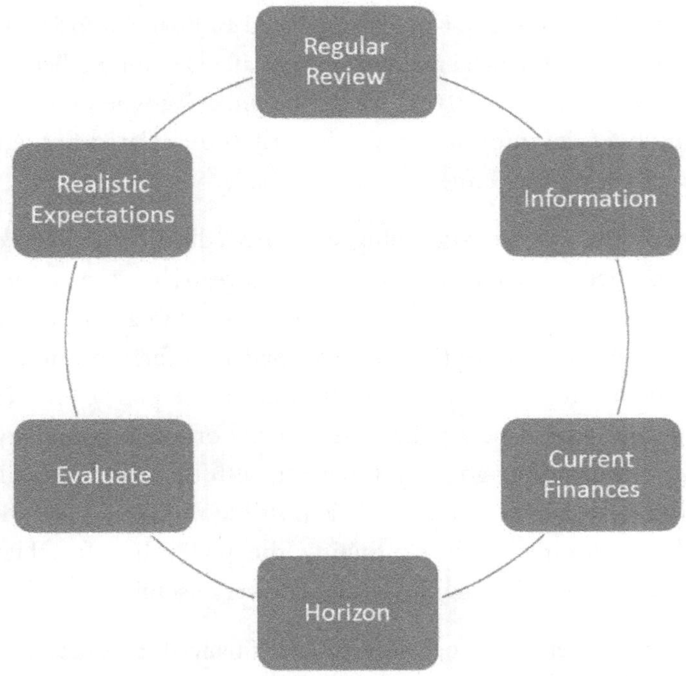

Illustration 3.4: RICHER

Let's look at the RICHER in a little detail, as it can make you richer:

1. Regular review

Doing a review just once in a quarter can yield you better results and help in keeping financial goals on track, with reference to economic environment as well as your own financials. The review is to be done with reference to the progress on achieving a selected financial goal. A few important parameters to be reviewed for a particular goal are:

a. Asset Allocation
b. Investment performance
c. Any Immediate action needed

2. Information

An individual who is not much interested in financial markets will also learn about financial markets once financial planning becomes a habit. On a serious note, you need to be proactive when it comes to seeking financial information, particularly those related to financial transactions and investments you have made.

For example, you are continuing with a Medical Insurance Policy with a particular insurance provider for 4-5 years, however, somehow you are not satisfied with the present insurer. What's to be done? Earlier there was no option but you had to either continue with the same insurer or get a new medical insurance policy with a new insurer; but with a new policy the benefits of owning a policy for 4-5 years will simply go away. However, with the new "portability", rule the same can be done, i.e. it is possible to take a policy from a different insurer while continuing the policy benefits. Having information about "portability" would be very useful.

Keeping & seeking information about financial products bought would help in maximising benefits. This can be done by reading product brochures, statement of investments and transactions, business newspapers, watching business news channels and business information websites. Please refer to the appendix for a list of business newspapers, business news channels and business websites.

3. Current finances

While planning for financial goals including prioritising them, one of the major factors (or constraints) is current financial condition. Over a period of time, financial conditions change, mostly improve. With the passage of time, owing to higher work experience, business expansion, added skills, and also due to lower liabilities and fulfilled financial goals, financial positions become healthier. With changes in current financial conditions, some of the constraints may become redundant and you may like to relook at asset allocation, participation in risky asset class, planning for other financial goals or maybe relook at the priority ranking.

For an example, at the time of financial planning, allocation of retirement planning was, say, ₹ 2500 based on financial condition and priority to the financial goal at the time of initiating this goal. Later on, with the passage of time and with the improved financial conditions you may like to increase the allocation to, say, ₹ 5000. This you would like to do due to better financials today and due to better life standards.

4. Horizon

Time horizon is a critical factor in financial planning. How much time (years or months) is remaining for a financial goal to materialise has an important bearing on strategy for the remaining period. Asset allocation, for example, would move from riskier asset class to conservative asset class as one moves closer to the selected financial goal.

To clarify further, for retirement planning, assume it is 15 years away from today. At present, you decide to invest in equity and debt-oriented investment in the ratio of 70:30 i.e. 70% equity-oriented investment and 30% debt-oriented investment. After 5 years (time to retire is now 10 years), you may like to change ratio to, say, 60:40 i.e. 60% equity-oriented investment and 40% debt-oriented investment. After another 5 years (time to retire is now 5 years) you may like to change ratio to, say, 30:70 i.e. 30% equity-oriented investment and 70% debt-oriented investment and when retirement is 2 years away, you may like to change to 100% debt-oriented investment and onwards you may like to add money market investment or cash equivalents.

Technically, with time horizon, asset allocation moves from wealth creation to wealth preservation as time progresses.

In the above example, there is the possibility that in other financial goals the asset allocation remains higher in equity-oriented investment, if time of maturity of the financial goals is also higher.

5. Evaluate

In the course of planning, regular review and re-planning, when it comes to implementing a particular financial decision, there comes a financial transaction. For example, for one of the financial goals you decide that investment should be in equity market and out of several choices, you decide and invest in a particular scheme of a mutual fund; this is a transaction.

Impact of a plan, effectiveness of planning, finally depends on efficiency of implementation. Therefore, before buying a product or entering into a financial transaction its impact needs to be assessed. Normally, it may be difficult to comprehend the product completely, though to ensure that selection of product is a good fit to the financial plan, do the due diligence that is necessary.

Asking following questions to your advisor or to yourself before initiating a transacting should help you in taking an informed decision. These questions are:

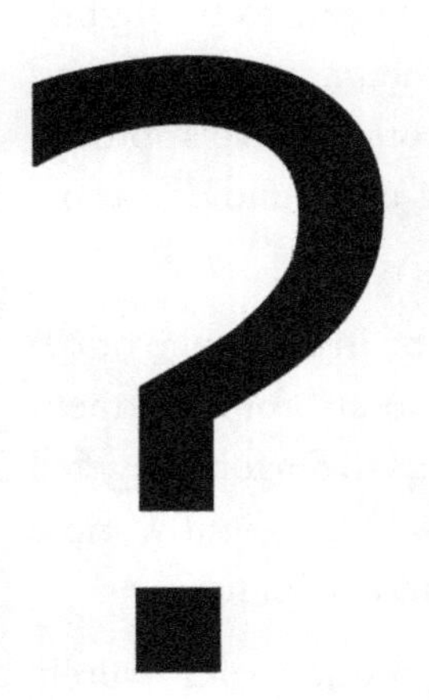

1. Why this?
2. How is it to be done?
3. How long?
4. How much?
5. What's the Return?
6. What's the alternative?
7. What's the tax implication?
8. What's the liquidity?
9. What are the charges?
10. What's the regulation?

By seeking answers to the above questions with reference to a particular transaction in context of selected financial goals, you will gain a deeper understanding. Seeking answers to these questions is also important because of the fact that when a product is chosen over other available alternatives, the reason for selection should be the features of the products. Lack of time or impulsive decision should not be the reasons for finalising a product.

The impact of selecting a product needs to be assessed from a variety of angles. A financial product, which has a tax savings element might have a longer lock-in period. So, if you foresee liquidity needs then this cannot be the right investment. On the other hand, if you have a longer horizon then investment with lock-in period with added tax benefit will add to your wealth.

6. Realistic expectations

Returns on a particular investment portfolio depends on Asset Allocation i.e. what mix of equity, debt, gold, cash etc. you have invested. Essentially, the asset allocation reflects (or should reflect) your risk profile. For practical purposes, when setting aside a sum for targeting a particular financial goal, it is prudent to be slightly conservative. This gives a marginal cushion to the financial goals and in case of returns being below expectation, a conservative approach will take care of targeted corpus at the time of need, and deviation, if any, will be within controllable limits.

For example, for debt asset class, returns could be in the range of 6% to 10%, depending on the product and tenure chosen. For investment estimation purposes, if returns are assumed to be, say, 8% for a targeted corpus, the amount of investment needed will be slightly more compared to the case when returns are assumed to be higher.

Gaining more knowledge about a financial product would surely help in assessing realistic return. Also, equally important is to comprehend the form of return on investment. For example let's consider an investment of ₹ 75000 in fixed deposit with a Bank for 3 years at a quarterly compounding 8% p.a. rate. There are two options the banker would ask, 1. Regular interest or 2. Interest reinvestment. In the first case, interest at a regular frequency, say every month, will be deposited in your savings bank account and at the time of maturity you shall get your investment of ₹ 75000 back. In the second case, you will get after 3 years ₹ 75000 with interest and in between there would not be any amount paid.

Option 1 – Monthly interest payment

Month	Amount	Remarks
0	(₹ 75000)	Investment made
1	₹ 500	Interest credit in savings bank account
2	₹ 500	Interest credit in savings bank account
3	₹ 500	Interest credit in savings bank account
-	-	-
36	₹ 75500	Investment matures

Option 2 – Interest Reinvestment

Month	Amount	Remarks
0	(₹ 75000)	Investment made
1	-	No intermediate interest payment
2	-	No intermediate interest payment
3	-	No intermediate interest payment
-	-	No intermediate interest payment
36	₹ 95118	Investment matures

In another example, say, in a performing mutual fund, your returns are in the form of investment and you get dividends and growth in the Net Asset Value (NAV). Dividend will be a source of regular (but only when declared) income while you will book gain on your capital when you redeem your investment partially or fully. So when estimations are made about future returns, both dividend and capital gains need to be considered including tax impact.

There are illustrations that will clarify returns calculations and taxations impact. At this point, for any investment, from return estimation point of view, it is important to understand form of return as well, so that return estimations are based on superior information, and forecasting can be well-defined and realistic.

As a caution, while investing in a product, you should avoid assuming future return based on "best" performance in the past including recent past. To estimate return on investment, the approach should be based on an intelligent estimate of the future performance and average performance over the longer tenure.

Goal-setting is the beginning of the financial planning process, and as it is said, financial goals should be SMART (Specific, Measurable, Actionable, Realistic and Time Bound).

If these SMART goals are supplemented with RICHER you can become RICHER, SMARTly.

4. What You Should Know: The God is in the Details

"The only reason for time is so that everything doesn't happen at once"
- Albert Einstein

Financial planning is a positive approach towards life goals. It is built on existing financials and systematically suggests ways to achieve desired goals. It's a journey from the level of today to a higher level of tomorrow. While the focus of this journey is to achieve decided life goals, it is important to know and analyse the present financial condition.

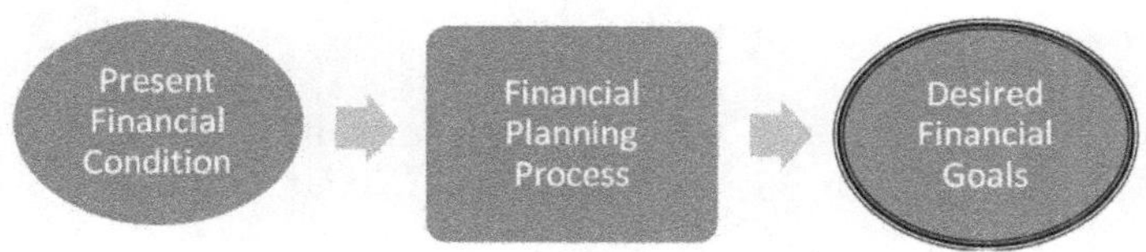

Illustration 4.1: Preparing for Financial Plan

Present financial conditions or present financial status is the base on which a financial plan will be built. On existing financial bases further financial planning is done. Let's assess current financial status by drawing Financial Statements.

1. Statement of Net Worth – Personal Balance Sheet

Net worth statement indicates accumulated income over a period of time. The income might have been invested and grown over a period of time, maybe in the form of various investments, property, gold, etc. Also, in the course of life, some liabilities might have been acquired like home loans, personal loans, outstanding credit card balances, etc. The Net worth statement shows excess of assets over liabilities. Higher the Net worth, the better it is. Though the value of Net worth depends on the life stage, with progress in life stage, net worth normally grows and it peaks at retirement.

Net worth shows the real worth, the net of loans & outstanding liabilities. Though concepts of corporate balance sheet preparation are not followed with regard to valuation of assets and liabilities, a few principles can help in assessing net worth on a particular date.

For example, let's say an individual has ₹ 10 lac worth of investment. So his net worth is ₹ 10 lac, assuming no other investments, liabilities, etc. for simplicity and to understand the impact of transaction.

Now, he uses this amount for buying a house for ₹ 35 lac with loan from a bank. Let's assume the amount is ₹ 25 lac. Assuming cost of house includes legal & registration charges also. Impact on net worth is:

Assets	House	₹ 35 lac (own amount ₹ 10 lac + loan ₹ 25 lac)
Less Liability	Loan	₹ 25 lac (loan from the Bank)
Net worth		₹ 10 lac

So, the net worth remains the same. An asset (House) was added and at the same time, a liability (Loan) was also added.

In this simple illustration, value of house was taken at the cost value since it was just acquired. On the date of preparation of Net worth statement, put present market value to the extent possible. There would be certain assets that are debatable on whether to include those in the list of assets for valuation purposes, for example, ornaments. In such cases it is advisable to use own judgment; as such there is no hard & fast method on an individual's net worth calculations.

Table no. 1

Asset No.	Assets	Amount, ₹	Narration
1	Cash in Hand		
2	Amount in Savings Bank a/cs		
3	Bank Fixed Deposits		
4	Market Value of Mutual Funds		
5	Gold & Ornaments		
6	House		
7	Other Assets		
	Total Assets		

Table no. 2

Liability No.	Liabilities	Amount, ₹	Narration
1	Housing Loan		
2	Auto Loan		
3	Personal Loan		

4	Credit Card Outstanding		
5	Personal Financial Guarantee		
6	Other Liabilities		
	Total Liabilities		

Net Worth = Total Asset – Total Liabilities

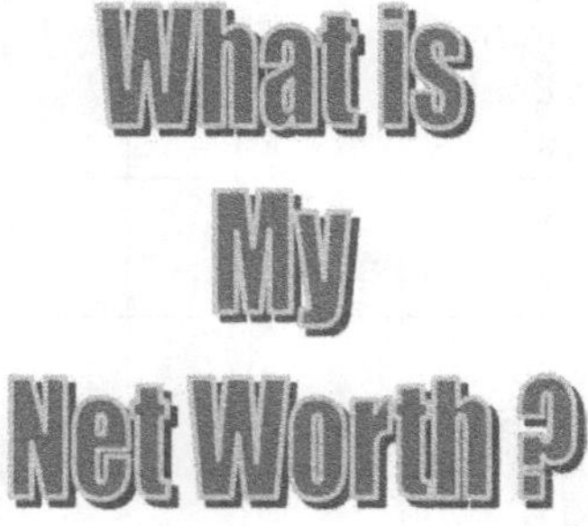

How much is good enough?

Net worth is an important indicator. Depending on age, net worth could be negative too, and this may so happen when liabilities viz. debts are higher than present value of assets. As one progresses in his or her career, net worth normally grows and in the later stage of life it grows exponentially. However, you can manage net worth proactively by managing assets and liabilities in a manner that increases the cash flow positively.

2. Income & Expenses Statement

Income and expenses statement is prepared based on monthly income and expenses. This is a statement which is close to a monthly budget. A detailed analysis of income and expenses statement will help you in saving a little more by rationalising expenses. This statement gives a fair picture about living standards, family's spending habits and most importantly, income & expenses snap shot with details that help in further analysis.

Income & expenses statement is prepared based on per month income or expenses under respective heads. It is better to divide income and expenses under distinct heads for better understanding and analysis. There are certain income heads as well as expenses that occur with irregular frequency or with frequency different than monthly. In such cases, average monthly figure or estimated monthly figure should be considered to make all numbers comparable.

Recognising a particular expense or income in the statement is a prerequisite. For example, buying jewelry is not an expense or paying an EMI on home loan is also not an expenses. Similarly, receipt from selling a plot of land is not an income. Need to remember that it is not a statement of cash flow or balance sheet. Also, this statement is to analyse income and expenses and not a statement prepared for income tax purpose.

Let's work it out.

Income Statement –

Table no. 3

Income No.	Income	Amount, ₹	Narration
1	Salary / Business Income		
2	Interest		
3	Dividend		
4	Rent		
5	Other Income		
	Total Income		

Expenses Statement –

Table no. 4

Expenses No.	Expenses	Amount, ₹	Narration
1	Rent		
2	Household Expenses		
3	Kids' Education		
4	Personal Expenses		
5	Other Expenses		
	Total Expenses		

Excess of income over expenses is savings, which is very critical for building the financial plan. Therefore, 'savings' will occupy centre stage of the discussion to achieve decided financial goals. Let's revisit the 'savings' equation

Savings = Income – Expenses

From the above calculations of income and expenses:

Savings Statement –

Table no. 5

S. No.	Particulars	Amount, ₹	Narration
1	Total Income		
2	Total Expenses		
3	Total Savings		(1) – (2)

For achieving financial goals, investment will be made from total savings as arrived in step (3) above.

There is a shortcoming to this approach; investment for achieving financial goals will be made from savings so arrived. The shortcoming is that investment amount available for achieving financial goals would depend on availability of funds leftover after expenses have been met. So every month, availability of amount will depend upon changes in expenses (assuming monthly income). This may so happen that in certain months savings could be lower than requisite investment amount. If this is the case, then investment for that month will be affected and that can jeopardise continuity of investment and financial goals.

We'll see how to manage savings in a much more prudent way.

3. Cash Flow Statement

Cash flow is a bit more elaborate than Income–Expenses Statement. It simply summarises cash in and cash out. In Income–Expenses statement, we consider regular income and for an individual the 'Cash In' is more or less the same except cash received for sale of an asset, gifts, bonus or other gains. However, the 'Cash Out' could be higher than expenses. The major use of cash is payment of EMI, credit card dues and above all, income taxes, which are independent of the level of your expenses.

Table No. 6

S. No.	Cash Flow	Amount, ₹	Narration
1	Total of Income in Table 1		
2	Proceeds from sale of Assets		
3	Cash from other sources		
4	Total Cash In		(4)= Sum of (1) to (3)
5	Total of Expenses in Table 2		
6	House Loan EMI		
7	Vehicle Loan EMI		
8	Credit Card Payments		
9	Income Tax		
10	Donation		
11	Home Repair, Car Repair		
12	Other Non-routine spending		
13	Total Cash Out		(13)=Sum of (5) to (12)
14	Net Cash Flow		(4) – (13)

The Net Cash Flow figure is the base for planning further towards achieving financial goals, if some of the goals, have already been planned. The amount which is set aside or invested will also become part of Cash Out.

We'll see how we can improve Net Cash Flow.

4. Know your Financial Status - Snapshot of your Finances

Let's continue to talk about your finances in further detail. Information gives an edge and knowing about yourself prepares for a robust foundation. After working on net worth and Income & Expenses, a little more analysis gives a clear-cut picture and prepares one better for financial planning foundation.

Some of the important parameters are grouped as given below:

A. Financial Strength

1. Net worth
2. Total Assets
3. Average Savings per month

B. Liquidity Position

4. Liquidity
5. EMIs/Income

C. Liabilities Assessment

6. HLV & Insurance Needed
7. Liabilities

D. Investment Assessment

8. Total Investment
9. Debt/Equity

E. Income Assessment

10. No. of Income Sources
11. Income Concentration

These terms are self-explanatory, but let's briefly describe these indicators and then proceed to calculate their values.

A. Financial Strength

This group indicates your financial worth as of today.

1. Net worth: This is the assets net of all liabilities and it is the worth on which you have a claim. Higher net worth is the aim for everyone and for which financial plans are being made.
2. Total Assets: Total of assets, as seen in the net worth statement (*Table no. 1*). The important part here is to have income generating assets, which helps in diversifying the income.
3. Average Savings per month: This is the average as in the income–expenses statement (*Table no 2*). Savings varies based on the life stage. For a young couple it would normally be less owing to buying property (home, car, etc.) on loan and as one progresses with higher income, it grows. In financial planning, the aim is to maximise the savings and then channelise these savings into productive investment. Please do remember, savings alone is not sufficient.

B. Liquidity Position

This group indicates liquidity position at any given time. Sometimes we say that liquidity position is tight; it does not mean lower financial strength but at the given time lower cash in hand or lesser amount of investment convertible to cash.

4. Liquidity: Liquidity is availability of cash when needed. It is number of times cash or cash equivalent compared to monthly expenses. Depending on income source, 3 to 6 times of monthly expenses is recommended to be kept in cash or

cash equivalent. In financial planning we plan for this too as we provide for emergency funding, which we'll see later. Managing liquidity is very important as less liquidity may lead to default on payment or liquidation of investment/fixed assets and higher liquidity means foregoing potential returns, as cash or cash equivalent earns no or minimal return.

5. EMIs/Income: This ratio is an indication of credit commitment. Improved credit score goes a long way in securing loans. A well-managed ratio will help in improving the same and one should ensure no default in EMI payments.

C. Liabilities Assessment

Liabilities assessment and provision for these liabilities is not only important for prudent financial management (cost as well as outstanding amount) but is also critical from family's financial security point of view. This is to be examined in context of what if the income source stops.

6. Outstanding Loans: Keep a close watch on total amount of outstanding debt and also cost (net of Taxes) of funding. Timely payment of principal and interest, depending on the repayment schedule of the loan is a must. Explore prepayment option or change in the loan portfolio if it is cost effective. For example, if you have an outstanding personal loan, which is normally a high cost loan (i.e. higher interest rate with no tax benefit) then explore if the loan against property can be availed, which may also be without tax benefits but comes with lower interest rates.
7. Other Outstanding Amount and Personal Guarantees: One of the heaviest outstanding loans is unpaid credit card debt and second in some cases could be short-term market borrowing from local money lenders. In fact, both of these so-called short-term borrowings end up in long-term high

cost debt, servicing of which is worrisome and interest cost is exorbitantly high. Another important point is Financial Guarantees given to business, relatives other than own family members and friends, which are often forgotten and considered as mere formalities. But in case when guarantees are invoked by the lending bank, it creates sudden and heavy dent on your finances. Be careful while giving guarantees and fully provide for it by considering it as liability till the time guarantee is in force.

8. HLV & Insurance needed: Human Life Value or HLV, though an old concept, can still can be considered as an indicator of capitalization of future Income. It is viewed as replacement value of present income sources or sources with lump sum money today. Insurance-needs assessments are based on Human Life Value. From this lump sum money, expenses of the family can be provided for in the unfortunate event that the breadwinner ceases to exist. Outstanding loan and other liabilities have a direct relationship with Life Insurance needs. Insurance requirement would be HLV + Outstanding Loan & Liabilities – Existing Investments & Assets other than living home.

D. Investment Assessment

Savings need to be channelised for productive purposes to generate higher returns, though one needs to keep liquidity in mind and that amount should be invested keeping in mind financial goals planned i.e. amount that might be needed at the time of need.

9. Total Investment: Investment portfolio is to be built carefully, keeping in mind that Investment Portfolios are designed to achieve financial Goals. One needs to keep watching the average return from an investment so made, more so if you have an outstanding loan too. In some cases, it is better to

prepay loan than continuing with the investment. And also, do evaluate net return while investing for tax purposes.

10. Debt/Equity ratio: One should make investments based on his or her risk profile. Having said that, it has been observed that many a time, actual investment made is different than risk profile and targeted financial goal. The ratio indicates actual investment to be compared with targeted Debt to Equity ratio.

E. Income Assessment

Well, we all strive to increase Income. The very goal of financial planning is to make money work for you to have a second income source.

11. No. of Income Sources: The answer to the question on how many sources of income you have is a simple but powerful answer. And, in case you are employed, you would have restrictions to take another or part time job. However, over a period of time, with financial planning a second income source in the form of well-planned portfolio can be built. In general, having more than one income source is needed, irrespective of current business or profession, and you should attempt to add one in a planned way.
12. Income Concentration – This indicates dependency on source of income calculated as below. For an individual who has only one source of income i.e. Income from source 1 is 100% then Income Concentration is $1^2 = 1.0$ or 100%

    For another individual who has three income sources, 60% of total income comes from source 1, 30% from source 2 and remaining 10% from the third.

    Income Source 1 – 60%, Income Source 2 – 30 %, Income Source 3 – 10%

Income Concentration = $0.6^2+0.3^2+0.1^2=0.46$ or 46%

> Lower value of the indicator is better. It indicates how diversified is the income source.

Let's calculate the value of these parameters to have the value of financial indicators for you.

Table No. 7

Financial Status No.	Financial Status Indicator	Value	Narration (How to Calculate)
A. Financial Strength			
1	Net worth		Net worth statement, difference between total assets and total liabilities
2	Total Assets		Total of *Table No. 1*
3	Average Savings per month		Average of *Table no. 6* (calculated for 3-4 months)
B. Liquidity Position			
4	Liquidity		(Total of Cash in Hand + Saving Bank A/c Balance)/Monthly Expenses
5	EMIs/Income		Total of EMIs/Total Income

C. Liabilities Assessment			
6	HLV & Insurance Needed		HLV = No of Years to Retirement (Assume 60 years) x Average Annual Income Insurance Needed = HLV + Liabilities & Guarantees – Assets excluding living home
7	Liabilities		Total of *Table no. 2*
D. Investment Assessment			
8	Total Investment		Total of Investment excluding Cash in hand & Savings bank A/c balance
9	Debt/Equity		Total Debt Investment Viz. Bank FD, Post office Deposit, Debt MF etc./ Total Equity Investment viz Shares, Equity MF, ELSS etc.
E. Income Assessment			
10	No. of Income Sources		Number of income sources 1, 2, 3 or as the case may be
11	Income Concentration		Sum of % squared

The end objective of all these calculations and analysis is to make money work for you, than you work for money. It is said that Money acts like a magnet and pulls more money. This is true, money can be invested to earn more money and the cycle goes on and you build strong sources of income and dependency reduces on single source of income.

The Next Step

With these calculations you have created a better foundation to prepare for financial planning. The next step is to build a financial plan, however let's make the foundation a little stronger by improving it.

Budgeting

Financial planning doesn't ask for curtailing of expenses, it only asks for prior planning. The budgeting will help in planning and providing for expenses. You will be amazed to see the power of provisioning.

The objective here is active Budgeting with an aim to increase the amount of net total savings (*Table no. 5*). First, analyze each and every item that appears in the expense table and see how it can be reduced and then follow the money mantra. Let's first see how expenses can be reduced with some examples.

Tracking expenses can give surprising results. Simply noting down all the expenses at the end of every day for about a month and then summarising to see where exactly money had been spent will tell you where to control expenses as well as to fine-tune the budget for subsequent months. Do not forget to include bills paid through credit cards or online banking and items bought on credit.

Tracking the expenses will also help you to explore other cost effective options, bargain on quantity if consumption is more, buying alternatively say online, negotiating for better rate etc. For example, if your consumption of gas cylinders in a year is more than the number of subsidised cylinders you get per year, then try to cut gas consumption and partly switch to electricity like induction cooking/

microwave to save on gas. Or there would be some expenses that occur once in two or three months, like cable recharge which can be provided monthly.

For some of the things you need to keep provision in anticipation, like gifts for weddings in the family circle or birthdays in the friend circle, etc. The essence here is to track and provide for every possible expense. As you progress, start budgeting for longer periods and stick to it by involving every member of the family.

Budgeting is a rewarding process, to give a clearer and holistic view of where money is coming from and how much you have and where exactly money is going. One thing to remember is that this is not a one-time process but a continuous one; keep exploring ways to reduce expenses without impacting the present standards of living. You will wonder when you realise how smaller expenses were eating up the bigger pie; controlling such expenses would add a lot to your home and wealth too.

If you observe people and family around you, you will find that people with good finances are those who are meticulous with their finances, manage their budget with discipline and are financially knowledgeable. Inculcate a few new habits, which will not occupy much of your time and resources, and will help you in building up financial strength.

1. Give about 2 hours once in a quarter to plan and budget and just half an hour every fortnight to track and review how your budgeting is working. Again, decide according to your work schedule, a day in the week for this and stick to it too.
2. Depending upon expense patterns, get knowledge about those expenses in detail and before you spend, get the full details of all the options available.
3. Read a lot about personal finance, which nowadays appears regularly in news dailies.

4. Avail advice of financial planners and if you are availing such service get the full benefit of it.
5. Discuss your budgeting plan with trusted friends and seek their advice if you feel the need to do so.
6. Keep exploring newer options as you grow in experience.

The Money Mantra –

Having a savings plan is the key. While budgeting you would have realised that more than income, it is important to have savings. Therefore, having a savings plan in place is a must. Savings as we all understood is leftover income, i.e.

Savings = Income – Expenses

Let's understand this with more clarity.

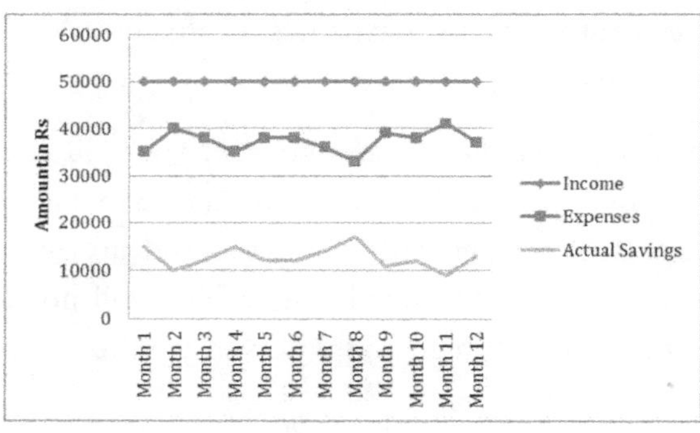

Amount in Rs	Month 1	Month 2	Month 3	Month 4	Month 5	Month 6	Month 7	Month 8	Month 9	Month 10	Month 11	Month 12
Income	50000	50000	50000	50000	50000	50000	50000	50000	50000	50000	50000	50000
Expenses	35000	40000	38000	35000	38000	38000	36000	33000	39000	38000	41000	37000
Actual Savings	15000	10000	12000	15000	12000	12000	14000	17000	11000	12000	9000	13000

Illustration 4.2: Savings vary month-on-month which impacts investment planning

If financial plans are based on average savings of ₹ 12000 a month, then in at least a couple of months, the amount available for investment would be lesser than needed.

In a nutshell, whatever is leftover is made available for investment, which could be equal than planned investment amount, or could be more or lesser.

The prudent approach will be to decide on targeted savings and then spend the leftover. With this, savings will always be certain and investment to the planned goals will always be as per the plan.

Expenses = Income – Targeted Savings

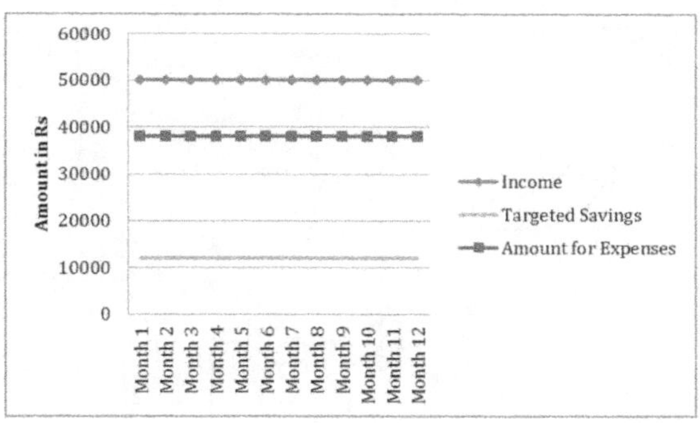

Amount in Rs	Month 1	Month 2	Month 3	Month 4	Month 5	Month 6	Month 7	Month 8	Month 9	Month 10	Month 11	Month 12
Income	50000	50000	50000	50000	50000	50000	50000	50000	50000	50000	50000	50000
Targeted Savings	12000	12000	12000	12000	12000	12000	12000	12000	12000	12000	12000	12000
Amount for Expenses	38000	38000	38000	38000	38000	38000	38000	38000	38000	38000	38000	38000

Illustration 4.3: Savings are known in advance which helps in Investment planning

The actual expenses may vary, however, one knows the amount available at his or her disposal beforehand.

A little change in approach can make a big difference in impacting the achievement of financial goals. This approach will add to more certainty in fulfilling desired financial goals.

Parameter to measure investment

For most of us, the amount so invested is hard earned money and saved with some sacrifice for a bigger cause. It is imperative to keep investments made under surveillance till the time it matures for the end use. One of the ways to classify investments is based on the LASER parameter; whenever you invest pass it through the LASER.

"Develop a
LASER sharp
eye before making
investment decisions"

What is LASER?

1. Liquidity 2. Accredited 3. Safety 4. Easy Operation and 5. Return

1. **Liquidity**
   The ease with which an investment can be converted to cash when needed is the measure of liquidity. Investments which are put in for a longer term with lock-in period will not be converted into cash when needed, however there could be the possibility of a loan. It is also a fact that high liquidity is

associated with lower returns, so one needs to balance in the context of overall portfolio liquidity and returns from the investment.

2. **Accredited**
   Investment, irrespective of promise of return and surety of principal repayment, you must see where it is accredited from. Government regulated schemes assure due diligence in terms of issuer and quality of investment (Inherent risk of the product remains, which is based on the nature of the product). For example, insurance products are regulated by IRDA; MF, PMS, Stock Markets etc. are regulated by SEBI; Bank Deposits, NBFC Deposits are regulated by RBI. Products that are not accredited will need to be probed in detail and one needs to be doubly sure before investing in, for example, buying physical gold or buying land or housing property.

3. **Safety**
   Safety of investment i.e. principal amount and interest earned so far must be ensured. This can be done with some due diligence of the investment. Most of the debt investments are rated by Credit Rating Agencies. Higher the rating, higher is the safety of principal and interest. Please refer appendix for credit ratings. A few equity products are also now graded which indicates quality of the investment, however, no rating completely indicates safety, since returns are linked to market performance. There are reviews available, which can be of help and there are private agencies which provide ratings of various products.

4. **Easy Operation**
   Given a choice of investments, you should select products that are easier to operate and are convenient. However statutory requirements e.g. KYC etc. must be followed.

5. **Return**

   Given the above parameters, you should obviously go for products that are expected to deliver the highest returns. As a thumb rule, investment, which delivers 4% above the bank deposit rate for the given tenure, should be reviewed with caution and risk factors should be analyzed in detail.

So, when you invest, pass it through the LASER test to make sure it qualifies as a prudent investment and gives you peace of mind.

Written Commitments

Finally to achieve on time and SMARTly, power of written commitment cannot be underestimated. Keep a record of all material financial transaction, maintain a file for filing paper documents, maintain soft copies whereever possible and keep a backup.

This will help in tracking your budget, planning further and for legal and other processes too, like filing IT returns or availing a loan.

5. How Financial Planning is Done: Draw a Life Picture

"Unless commitment is made, there are only promises and hopes; but no plans"
- Peter F. Drucker

Let's take a step closer to financial planning and planning for desired financial goals. The essence of financial planning is realistic achievement of desired financial goals. It's a journey and it is surely a pleasurable journey. The day you embark upon this pleasurable journey, it will add to knowledge, clear decisions, sense of accomplishments and above all, certainty.

Financial planning is the culmination of various decisions including selection of best-fit alternatives among choice of solutions available. It requires adequate knowledge and substantial experience before a best-fit solution is arrived at. For example, returns from Equity Markets beat returns from other financial asset classes. However, risk associated with equity markets need to be understood first before allocating funds to this asset class and you also need to understand life stage of the financial goal as well.

As said earlier, suitability of a financial plan and its execution is your own decision but you can make it better by your own experience or with an expert's advice. To make your decision better and to utilise the advisory to the fullest, some of the technical terms need to be understood. We'll work towards this and with some experience you shall comprehend these terms with ease. Only condition is commitment to fulfil selected financial goals. In the matter of financial planning, a few of the financial terminologies need to be understood correctly. It is quite likely that actual meaning of some of these terms may be different than you perceive generally. Therefore, sometimes, sequence of understanding becomes 'unlearning' first and learning later.

Let's work towards this.

How to select an alternative from the available choices of alternatives? Let's take a few illustrations to see the impact of decision so taken.

Consider two investment alternatives (subject to suitability as per your risk profile) that are available for a long period like post office deposit, bank fixed deposit, and corporate deposits, etc.

Let's take annual investment of ₹ 12000 every year (₹ 1000 per month) for a period of 10 years.

Alternative #1: Rate of Interest 8% p.a. compounding annually (pre-tax return, example bank deposit)

Alternative #2: Rate of Interest 12% p.a. compounding annually (pre-tax return; example, balance fund of a mutual fund)

Amount in ₹

Year	8 % Investment	12% Investment	Difference
1	60,000	60,000	0
2	124,800	127,200	2,400
3	194,784	202,464	7,680
4	270,367	286,760	16,393
5	351,996	381,171	29,175
6	440,156	486,911	46,756
7	535,368	605,341	69,973
8	638,198	737,982	99,784
9	749,253	886,539	137,286
10	869,194	1,052,924	183,730
11	998,729	1,239,275	240,546
12	1,138,628	1,447,988	309,360
13	1,289,718	1,681,747	392,029
14	1,452,895	1,943,556	490,661
15	1,629,127	2,236,783	607,656
16	1,819,457	2,565,197	745,740
17	2,025,014	2,933,020	908,007
18	2,247,015	3,344,983	1,097,968
19	2,486,776	3,806,381	1,319,605
20	2,745,718	4,323,147	1,577,429

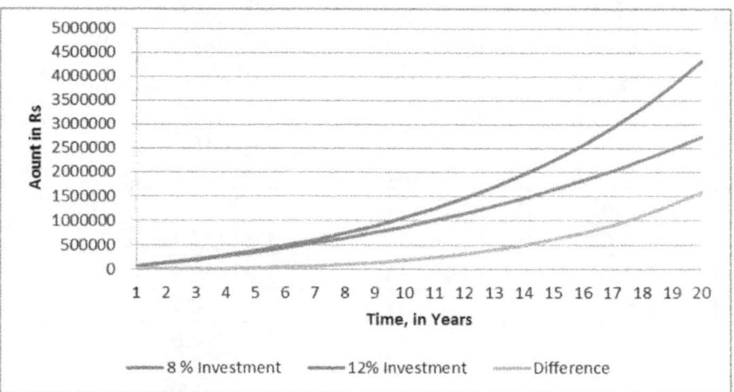

Illustration 5.1: The difference is substantial over a longer horizon

Longer the horizon, higher is the difference and over a period of time, the difference is too substantial to consider a safer alternative. Therefore, select an alternative that is a 'Good Fit' to financial planning horizon, i.e., invest in an alternative for a short term which is meant for short term and for a longer tenure investment select an alternative which is meant for longer term.

Inflation & Real Rate of Return: Even post-tax return is not real rate of return. In a true sense, investment return should be able to give returns above inflation. If post-tax return is above inflation then you are earning real return.

Amount in ₹

Year	6% (Inflation)	12% Investment	Real Rate of Return
1	60,000	60,000	60,000
2	124,800	127,200	123,402
3	194,784	202,464	190,399
4	270,367	286,760	261,195
5	351,996	381,171	336,004
6	440,156	486,911	415,056
7	535,368	605,341	498,589
8	638,198	737,982	586,859
9	749,253	886,539	680,134
10	869,194	1,052,924	778,698
11	998,729	1,239,275	882,850
12	1,138,628	1,447,988	992,908
13	1,289,718	1,681,747	1,109,206
14	1,452,895	1,943,556	1,232,097
15	1,629,127	2,236,783	1,361,957
16	1,819,457	2,565,197	1,499,180
17	2,025,014	2,933,020	1,644,184
18	2,247,015	3,344,983	1,797,409
19	2,486,776	3,806,381	1,959,322
20	2,745,718	4,323,147	2,130,416

Real Rate of return = (1 + R) / (1+i) – 1 = 1.12/1.06 – 1 = 5.67% (it's not 12% - 6% = 6%)

For the longer-term horizon, do provide for Inflation and select an alternative that gives a higher real rate of return.

These are some possible situations, which you may come across while deciding on an alternative from the available choices of investment vehicles, for attainment of given financial goals. Essentially, before deciding on an investment, your decision should ideally follow these two principles:

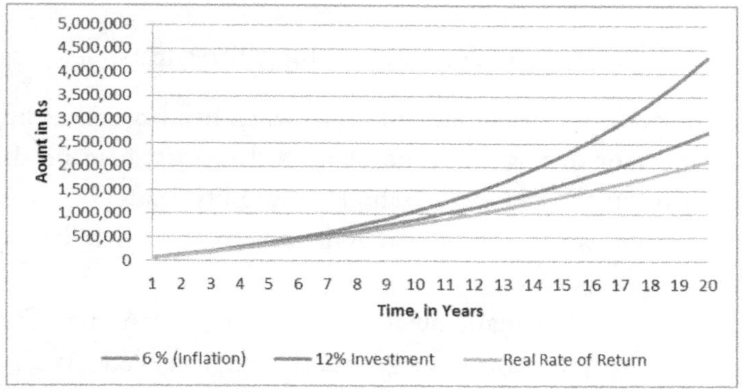

Illustration 5.2: Real rate of return from investments is lower than absolute return

1. **10-10-10 Rule (give at least 10 hours in evaluating 10 alternatives for 10 years investment option)**
   The idea is to evaluate from all possible angles before finalising one or more for your investments. Longer the investment horizon, the better it is to spare more time to evaluate all the options. Though, irrespective of the tenure or investment horizon, investment options need to be evaluated with utmost diligence. However, when the investment horizon is longer and the investment vehicle is altered mid-way, then opportunity cost is higher.

2. **Compare post-tax return**
   This is essential for the simple reason that "net earning" matters more than gross earning. A product with say 8% p.a. tax free returns could be better than 9% p.a. taxable return for an individual who falls in 20% tax slab. For him, the "net return" is 7.2% (9% x (1-0.2) = 7.2% subject to cess). The product, which apparently delivers more, actually provides

returns lower owing to taxation. Another important aspect of taxation is that a few products are taxed at the source itself, these products are generally advantageous for individuals in higher tax brackets than those in lower tax brackets. Post tax return is a better metric to compare product returns.

And check that product so selected clears these three tests:

3. **Liquidity** is the availability of funds when needed at the end of tenure or during the time of need. Liquidity also needs to be optimally planned, as higher liquidity leads to lower returns and lower liquidity may lead to non-availability of funds when needed.
4. **Certainty** is the main purpose of financial planning. The objective of planning is to get funds when needed. At the time of need, the fund so available should be protected from risks, to get the amount so planned.
5. **Risk** is to be understood clearly and then it must be within acceptable limits during period of planning for a particular goal. Also, total risk should be within limits as per your risk profile.

Having prepared the background for selecting "Best Fit" alternative, now let's go through the financial planning process. Why financial planning process at this juncture? Well, financial planning process is quite an elaborate one and it encompasses various decisions regarding investment amount, investment product, risk, liquidity and so on, including availability of product at a given point. Therefore, it is an iterative process and before arriving at a "Best Fit" solution, quite a good number of permutations and combinations need to be evaluated. Looking at importance of financial goals too, a sincere and serious evaluation is needed to conclude on an investment alternative. So, we are at a stage where we'll talk about financial goals and we'll quantify them. The financial planning process will further assist in comprehending the whole process of deciding a financial goal and help in preparing a road map to achieve them.

We can compare the financial planning process with preparing the main course dinner, to comprehend importance of preparation. Even though the ingredients to prepare the main course are standardised, the quantity of ingredients, your experience in cooking and the way you cook makes all the difference. Those who love good food get their food prepared with diligence to get the taste they want. In the same way, you would like to manage your own finances meticulously to get the value of every single rupee earned and saved for future goals planned.

The financial planning process is highly individualistic and reflects an individual's approach to his or her own finances with the end result of achievement of planned financial goals. Therefore it is also referred to as personal financial planning. On theoretical grounds, financial planning as a process involves setting up financial goals, prioritising them, deploying from existing financial resources to diligently selected financial products, with control on finances as planned and regular review, and continuously repeating this process. Practically, it's achievement of enhanced economic position from existing financial resources.

Therefore, financial plan depends on:

1. **Present Financial Situation**
   Savings, obligations, liabilities, monthly income, existing investment and employment benefit (if employed).

2. **Financial Goals to be Achieved**
   Amount needed, when needed, cash flow requirements (e.g. one time or regular), financial protection.

3. **Priority of Financial Goals**
   Education, Marriage, Home, Leisure, etc.

4. **Your Point of View on Risk for Selection of Financial Products**
   Debt or equity orientation, how many years to achieve a particular financial goal.

5. **Other Factors**
   Discipline in controlling finance, age, number of dependents in the family, knowledge of finance.

Every financial plan is unique due to the simple fact that all these factors are different for different individuals, hence there cannot be one solution to fit to all. However, the process of arriving at a solution that is unique to an individual can always be suggested. The end result, however, is the same – achievement of financial goals, stability and much lower uncertainty of achieving major life goals, and satisfaction of optimising financial resources and finally achieving the financial freedom, which is the main purpose of the whole financial planning process – to make money work for you.

Steps in creating a financial plan for you:

Step # 1: Decide Financial Goals

Step # 2: Assess Current Financial Situation

Step # 3: Prioritise Goals Based on Step 2 Above

Step # 4: Decide on a Comprehensive Investment Plan

Step # 5: Implement the Plan

Step # 6: Review, Monitor and Repeat from Step 1

Let's begin with **Step#6**, which also is a repeat from step 1. Since financial planning is a continuous process, one may need to repeat the process at regular intervals till the financial goals are achieved. This is so for a variety of reasons, mainly due to the fact that underlying financial situation can vary drastically and also, as time progresses

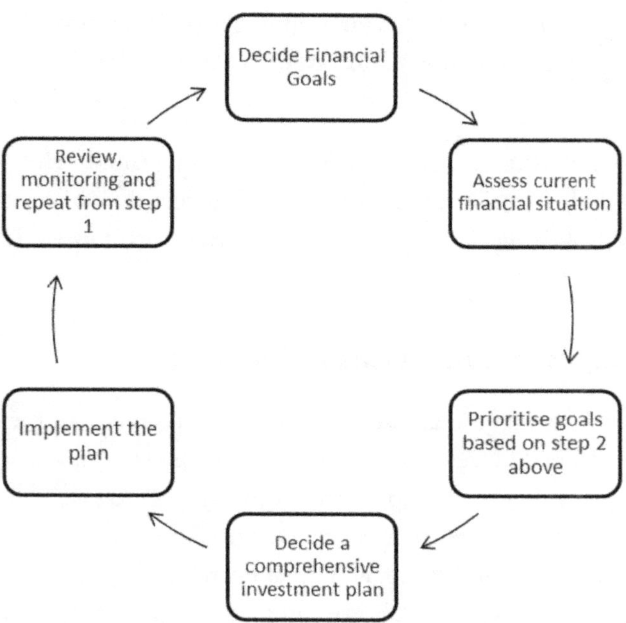

Illustration 5.3: Steps in creating a Financial Plan

efficiency of implementation of the plan also goes up. This will also be clarified as we progress.

Step # 1: Decide Financial Goals

This is the first step for the reason that once you decide targets, it is easier to gather resources to achieve that and it gives clarity to what is aimed at in the years to come. Depending on life stage, your life goals may vary. Major financial goals are education for kids, marriage for kids, home, retirement, foreign travel, car etc.

Once all the goals are decided, you need to quantify them with respect to when it is needed while considering inflation. For instance, assume that parents need to secure admission in a college for their kid 10 years from now. Also assume that the amount needed if the admission is taken today, is ₹ 10 lac. In this, the parents need to plan for ₹ 10 lac adjusted for inflation after 10 years, i.e., they will need approximately ₹ 18 lac (assuming 6% p.a. inflation). Therefore, financial goal (education) and target is to get ₹ 18 lac in 10 years' time.

Similarly, all the financial goals will be quantified with amount needed and with the targeted time. A Financial Goal Sheet will be of help in writing down your financial goals with targeted amount and targeted date.

Step # 2: Assess Current Financial Situation

This is to make an assessment of your income and expenses budget. If needed, rework on budget and forecast on conservative basis expected annual income in coming years. Assess realistically present and expected expenses and potential savings for the purpose of achieving planned financial goals. From savings, an investment plan will be made to achieve financial goals. Also, categorise existing assets into categories like liquid assets, investments and other fixed assets (refer to Table no. 3/Chapter 3), which gives clarity to deploy and align these assets and investment for planned financial goals.

Step # 3: Prioritise Goals Based on Step # 2 Above

With the financial goals ready with you, it may so happen that all the goals may not be initiated at once. Therefore, goals so selected need to be given ranking based on priority and for top priority goals an investment plan should be made. There are two ways to prioritise selected financial goals:

A. Importance of goals to the family like education for kids, marriage, or it could be buying a home, depending on the family's necessity. Based on this, you may categorise a goal as a High Priority Goal or Low Priority Goal.

B. Time priority is based on remaining time; in financial planning, time is the key resource and you should plan early. However, in case of a particular goal, if time availability is less, it will get higher rank and come up in the list of priorities, for example, paying for a certain liability. Based on this, you may call a goal a Short Term Goal or Long Term Goal.

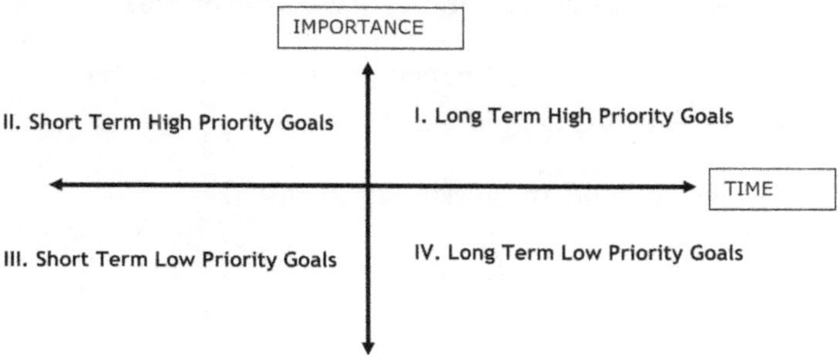

Illustration 5.4: Goal categorization based on Importance and available time

I. Long Term High Priority Goals: With prior and early planning, you will need lower resources to achieve your financial goals or with given resource you would be able to achieve more financial goals.

II. Short Term High Priority Goals: These goals put stress on your plan, early planning can avoid these. You may need to liquidate existing investment or may need to borrow to complete these goals.

III. Short Term Low Priority Goals: For financial goals falling in this category one may look at two options - first, if the amount can be varied and second, opportunity cost if these goals are postponed.

IV. Long Term Low Priority Goals: With time in your favour, one can plan for these goals with lesser resources. Again, you need to make sure that non-achievement of these goals should not have higher opportunity cost.

These priorities may change, owing to changing financial environment or availability of a suitable opportunity for lower priority goals. For fine-tuning financial goals, you can take inputs from those who have experience or seek financial portals for more information or talk to a financial advisor.

Step # 4: Decide on a Comprehensive Investment Plan

Having worked on prioritising financial goals, the next step is to select from available investment alternatives.

There are two ways to build an investment plan.

Goal-Based Approach

It is a goal-wise investment plan in which you select asset allocation and investment products for a particular goal. It means, for each of the financial goals you would separate asset allocation and also separate investment products. This will lead to more investment products, more accounts to handle but better clarity would be there in terms of achievement of the financial goals. It also gives clear mental accounting, and achievement or non-achievement of one financial goal does not affect other financial goals.

Common Portfolio Approach

In common portfolio approach you invest in a common pool with pre-decided asset allocation for all the financial goals, and investment is also pooled in selected investment products for a financial goal. Additional investment is made in same investment product by incremental investment. This approach is simple to maintain and manage. The disadvantage of this approach is to compensate for non-achievement of a goal from other goals' money.

While we shall learn about investment products in a later chapter, at this juncture it is imperative to categorise investment also known as asset classes.

1. Equity
2. Debt
3. Alternate
4. Cash Equivalent

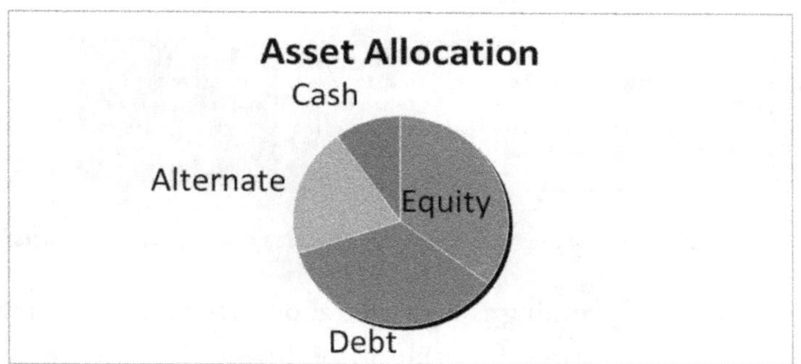

Illustration 5.5 : Asset allocation

When you divide your investment in these categories of assets, it is known as asset allocation.

Knowing asset allocation is key to investment decisions, and also important to understand the role expected from a chosen investment vehicle. As explained in the chart below, for a longer-term financial goal, one should look at wealth appreciation strategy; risk would be highest for this strategy, however, it has potential for highest returns too. These strategies are dynamic for a chosen goal. As a financial goal approaches the time of realisation, you would need the requisite money with certainty, therefore you should move asset allocation more towards debt, and towards the end of the financial goal, asset allocation will be more in cash equivalents.

Possible Asset Allocation

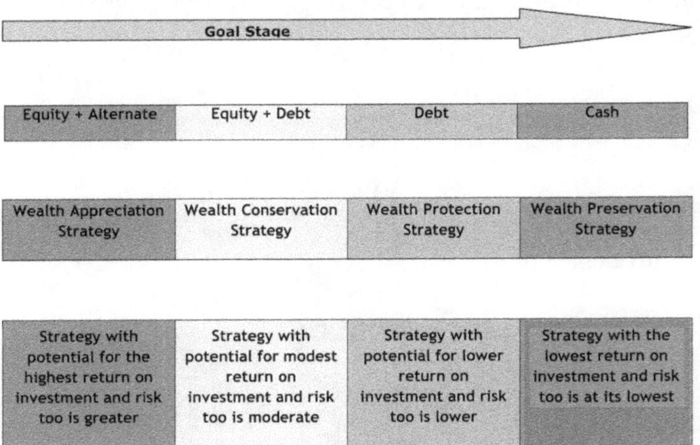

Goal Stage
Equity + Alternate
Equity + Debt
Debt
Cash
Wealth Appreciation Strategy
Wealth Conservation Strategy
Wealth Protection Strategy
Wealth Preservation Strategy
Strategy with potential for the highest return on investment and risk too is greater
Strategy with potential for modest return on investment and risk too is moderate
Strategy with potential for lower return on investment and risk too is lower
Strategy with the lowest return on investment and risk too is at its lowest

Illustration 5.6: Dynamics of asset allocation, with relative risk and return potential

In the Goal-Based planning as suggested above, a separate investment portfolio will be prepared for each of the financial goals. Hence it may so happen that in one of the financial goals you are going for wealth preservation and in other portfolio for wealth appreciation. The entire portfolio of investment is designed according to your risk profile. So, for example, if you have 6 financial goals, then you would have 6 investment portfolios. In this approach, a change in one of the goals will not impact other goals.

As we progress, you will be able to design a portfolio for chosen financial goals. At this point it is also important to add that for all these portfolios, the investment amount would come from the breadwinners' income. Practically, one needs to provide for a situation in case breadwinners cease to exist. In this unfortunate scenario, all the planning would be jeopardised and family would be severely affected. Life insurance is an answer to this. Adding adequate life insurance to the investment plan makes it complete and certainty is added with the insurance that chosen financial goals will be achieved.

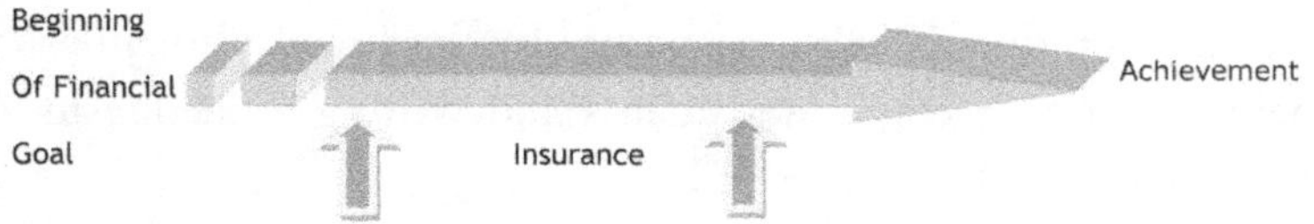

Illustration 5.7: Importance of Insurance in achieving financial goals

Based on selected financial goals, you should enlist all the available investment options, evaluate the alternative and shortlist investment products and add adequate insurance.

Step # 5. Implement the Plan

Implementing a plan is the most critical of all the steps in financial planning. This is so for the simple reason that all plans remain mere plans unless implemented. In my experience too I have found that a majority of the clients find this task the most formidable one. This is the challenge in mind to implement, the resistance comes from the tendency to verify the plan again to see that whether planning would give desired result or not. Prior to this step, planning and analysis remains on paper and from this step onwards commitment of resources commences towards fulfilment of planned financial goals.

What's the meaning of implementation? It's acting upon the financial plan so prepared. This comes after evaluating financial products & insurance plans which meet or are close to your requirements- legal requirements like KYC; banking requirements like opening an account, ECS etc.; holistically understanding the financial product including ways to operate it and its continuity, risks associated with it, and in case you come across a better option than the current financial product under consideration, an exit option with opportunity cost, performance parameters, product communication and ways to receive updates, i.e., email, SMS or personal meeting of financial advisor in case product is being suggested by the financial planner and finally signing necessary documents and writing a cheque to commence financial plan so planned.

In this process you may need the assistance of financial advisors who may facilitate transactions in addition to suggesting a financial product to you, or that you may need brokers for real estate, insurance, shares, mutual funds etc.

In my opinion, it is best to take assistance from a financial advisor, be it an individual or a firm. They will charge for their advice and in return you will get professional assistance which is better due to their professional qualifications and experience, and they are trained to suggest a wider gambit of financial products. If you are worried about the fact that they will maximise their commission at the cost of your investment, then ask them about the commission or brokerage they would be earning on the transaction. A transparent dealing will instil confidence in you and professional advice will help in building a sound financial plan. Moreover services needed during the currency of the financial plan can also be well taken care of by your financial advisor.

Step # 6. Review, Monitor and Repeat from Step 1

Final goals so planned and implemented are key milestones in your life which not only add to certainty as well as financial freedom, but these are the goals which must be achieved, therefore you would like to see that these are achieved without any deviation. With proper planning and comprehensive implementation there is no reason why planned goals are not achieved. To ensure further that these goals are achieved one would always keep track of it. Steps discussed from

1st to 5th step are the beginning, and as said, well begun is half done; literally step 1st to 5th are half the things done and the remaining half is continuous monitoring of implemented plans, regular reviews and repeating steps 1 to 5 at a pre-decided interval to accommodate changes in underlying situations, both internal to you and the external financial environment.

Why repeat steps 1 to 5 at a regular interval or when there is substantial change in underlying situations? Regular reviews will keep you updated, monitoring will ensure execution is on track and revisiting steps 1 to 5 will ensure that your financial plan reflects your current living standards and aspirations. Significant underlyings which will call for changes in your financial plans are:

A. Income Level - Changes in income level would impact allocation to financial plan; for higher income, allocation can be increased to achieve goals faster and then follow wealth preservation strategy. Also, more goals can be added in the financial plan to have clear goal oriented investments.

B. Risk Tolerance – Tolerance for risk changes based on your experience. Mostly with experience and knowledge, risk tolerance grows. Also, risk tolerance depends on the time remaining till the goal completion date. More the time available, higher could be the risk tolerance and vice-versa.

C. Priorities – Which goal should be given priority may change once sufficient amount is accumulated or when situation so arises.

D. Revisit Goals – With the passage of time new financial goals emerge, and this could be due to higher income level, changes in the family, change in profession, aspirational goals, experience or any other underlying factors which can cause changes in the financial goals.

E. Financial Markets – Investing assumptions are made regarding expected performance of the financial market. Assumptions with

Illustration 5.8 Financial Planning is an ongoing process

regard to returns and inflation may be different than expected, either in favour or against you. This will lead to review of the asset allocation and this may also lead to changes in the investment allocation to high priority goals too.

F. Taxation – Changes in taxation could compel you to look at alternative options. A new scheme with tax benefits may offer more attractive post tax returns than existing investments. In such a case you may like to switch to the newer investment option, or allocate some funds to such an investment, or make incremental investment to the extent tax benefit is available. In some cases, the existing scheme which had offered tax benefits may change. Change in taxation may impact outstanding loans' cost also, therefore changes in underlying taxation will need to revisit financial plan once.

Written Financial Plan

Financial planning is an important part of your life. The financial plan must be written and its sanctity must be maintained. This is the set of documents which creates a strong foundation to make a prosperous and safe financial future. Spend time in planning, gathering financial information; learn from others, consult financial planners, attend seminars, fine-tune financial goals and do take time to understand more on financial planning, but once you have decided on a financial plan, make a plan in writing and then stick to it till goals are achieved. Change the plan as required but in the process never abandon it; commit time as you originally planned. The result of this commitment is goal fulfilment and precious satisfaction.

Please refer to annexure **(Part II - A Financial Plan Written Commitment)** for the written statement of your financial plan.

Goal Sheet Form (Fill to enlist your financial goals)

S.No.	Financial Goal	When to Achieve (Month-Year)	Amount Needed Today	Amount Needed at Maturity	Priority Ranking

6. Some Technical Stuff: Know to Earn More

"Good fortune is what happens when opportunity meets with planning"
- Thomas Alva Edison

Knowing something new will always help in keeping you updated with the latest, and will keep your confidence level high too. If this new thing is financial concepts then it will help in taking more informed decisions and it will help in building more wealth too. In financial planning it is all the more important to know a few technical things for the simple reason that in the longer run, benefits of informed decisions would be handsomely rewarding.

Let's revise a few concepts which will assist you in making more informed decisions.

Concept # 1: Risk and Return Go Hand in Hand

There is irony when it comes to risk and return; for higher returns you need to take higher risks but merely taking higher risks doesn't mean that you will get higher returns. Therefore understanding risk and return is crucial for achieving your financial goals. Not only this, if the outcome is negative, i.e., you bear a loss completely on your own but in case of a positive outcome, i.e., positive returns you need to pay taxes. Therefore you also need to know the form of return so that tax can be assessed (tax is certain.)

A fair understanding of risk is essential for preparing and implementing a financial plan. Once you know about the risk then you may look at controlling and managing the risk. Risk is the probability of loss, and it is not just about the decision to take risks in case of investment. It is not just about allocating funds to riskier assets.

Mathematically speaking, risk is deviation from expected outcome. In simple terms, risk is the possibility of an outcome different than originally thought. If the actual outcome is different than the expected outcome then it is a risk. In financial planning therefore, risk if narrowly defined, is the possibility that the amount so planned is different than originally planned. For example you planned for ₹ 10 lac after 10 years and after 10th year you get amount ₹ 11 lac or ₹ 9.5 lac, since amount is different than originally planned it's a risk. Returns higher than expected is also a deviation and hence a risk!

However, in this example we are not worried if we get more (provided there is no opportunity cost) so we are only worried about cases where there is a possibility of the outcome amount being lesser than expected or originally planned. Therefore, since we are concerned about the downside, i.e., lower than expected return risk in practical sense is the probability of lower than expected return. It means that the maturity amount that you expect from your investment for a particular goal will fall short of the targeted amount.

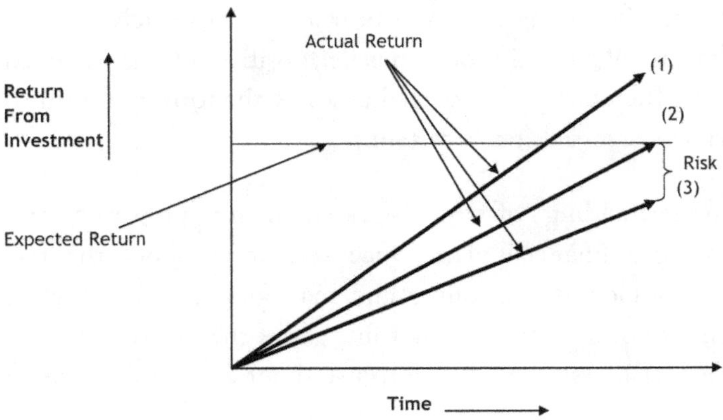

Illustration 6.1: Risk, practically, is the probability of unfavorable outcome

(1) Actual Return > Expected Return, Favorable Outcome

(2) Actual Return = Expected Return, Expected Outcome

(3) Actual Return < Expcted Return, Unfavorable Outcome hence the Risk

Continuing with the example, risk is getting 0.5 lac lesser than planned. This is the risk and risk amount is ₹ 0.5 lac. This is a simpler explanation of the risk. Your financial advisor should be more equipped with the risk and should give you suggestions on how to handle this.

Before we go further on risk, let's see what are some possible causes of getting a smaller amount than expected:

1. Inflation – You need an amount more than originally planned due to higher cost, therefore though you could save and invest, inflation may have turned out to be higher than expected.

2. Investment Amount – Amount contributed reduces to less than needed due to change in income or breadwinner ceases to exist.

3. Rate of Return – Return is different than planned or needed. In the first case, the product selected did not perform as expected

due to financial market conditions or product's performance but return is lesser than expected in former selection of product or asset allocation was not appropriate. To explain further, the product can give 8% p.a. return whereas need was 8.5% p.a.

4. Taxation – It may also happen that the taxation rule may have changed, which would have impacted post - tax returns adversely.

Out of these four reasons viz inflation, investment amount, rate of return and taxation, the major component is rate of return and this requires a little elaboration. Rate of return is linked with asset allocation and aligning asset allocation with the risk profile, and tenure of financial goal would make sure that expected returns are on expected lines. Investments are made to achieve chosen financial goals and aligning asset allocation to chosen financial goals is the wiser investment policy, and a prudent way to mitigate the risk. On the contrary, selecting asset allocation which is conservative will lead to lesser risk but would result in lower returns. On the other hand, impulsive investment based on tips or rumours will lead to disproportionately higher risk which may cost principal amount. Therefore, investing in an appropriate asset allocation that is in alignment with the financial goal is an objective way to manage the risk.

The fact remains that the risk cannot be completely eliminated; it can be controlled and managed. You can look at the following ways of dealing with the risks in investments.

1. Bear the Risk – Particularly when the expected loss is not much and it makes sense to retain the risk and bear the loss in case it occurs. These are low frequency low loss events.

2. Transfer the Risk – Risk of incurring cost on medical treatment, which can jeopardise your savings and investment plans can be managed through medical insurance and similarly life of the bread winner can be insured to protect the family's financial interest at

least. This way, risk will be transferred to the insurance company and financial plans will not be impacted much in case of any eventuality.

3. Avoid the Risk – Don't venture where there is risk. Completely avoid any risky activity that could lead to financial loss.

The major learning with regard to risks is to know the risk and provide for it to ensure that financial plans reach their destination with certainty, without any hurdle and on time.

In our quest to manage risk, let's look at a tradeoff between risk and return and we shall see a few ways to do the same, but before that let's look at the return and consider some examples to understand the return.

Example # 1 - You had invested in a residential plot for ₹ 6 lac and after 4 years you sell it for ₹ 10.5 lac, the difference of ₹ 4.5 lac is realised return. The absolute return is 75% and annual compounding return is 15% p.a.

Example # 2 - You deposit ₹ 100000 in a bank for 3 years, which pays you 8.5% p.a. quarterly compounding interest. The interest is credited monthly to your savings bank account and you withdraw ₹ 100000 on maturity.

Example # 3 - You buy 1000 shares of a company at the rate of ₹ 75 per share and you sell it for ₹ 100 in 2 years, during the period the company pays a dividend of ₹ 5 and ₹ 6 respectively in year 1 and year 2.

In the above examples, the nature of investment returns are different. In example # 1 you get appreciation in capital with no intermittent income. In example # 2 you get only intermittent interest income with no appreciation in capital. In example # 3 you get both intermittent income and capital appreciation.

In general, return from an investment can be realised in three forms:
1. Capital appreciation as in example #1
2. Interest income as in example #2
3 Dividend income as in example #3

For an investment you may have a combination of the above, for example if you invest in a bond which is listed on the exchanges, then you get interest and you may also get capital appreciation. Knowing forms of return is important to comprehend a financial instrument and to assess expected return. More importantly, taxation depends on what form of return you get, so it will further help you in tax planning.

How to manage the risk and maximise expected return: balancing risk and return -

At the risk of repeating myself, let me say that when the risk in the underlying is low, then the expected return will also be low. When the underlying risk is high, then the expected return will also be high. However, it only indicates a probability of higher returns and does not guarantee it. Since risk means probability of loss or less than expected returns and low risk means low potential returns, something is needed which balances risks for chosen financial goals and expected returns.

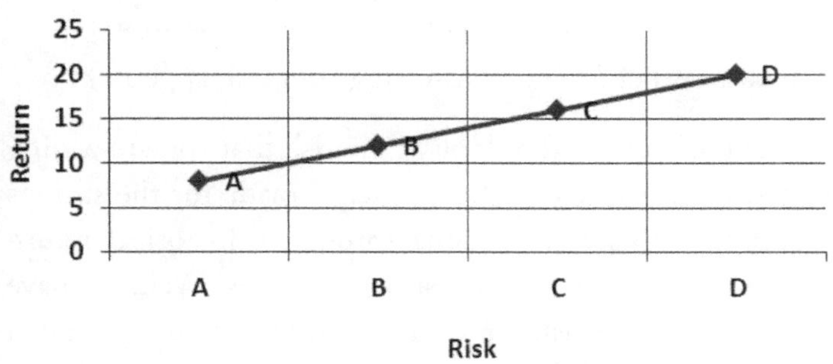

Illustration 6.2 : Risk –Return relationship

A. Ranging from savings bank deposits, money market instruments, CDs, short term bank deposits, endowment plans

B. Traded Bonds, term deposits, NCDs, MF- debt funds, FMPs, ULIP-debt

C. Large cap stocks, MF- equity funds, ULIP – equity funds

D. Midcap – small cap stocks, MF – sectoral funds

At the beginning of the risk-return line you have sovereign securities backed by the Government of India and it goes up progressively, with increased risk, average potential return also goes up.

Indicative Portfolio based on your risk appetite:

Portfolio	Asset Allocation
Low Risk	100% Cash, Cash Equivalents, Money Market, Govt. Securities
Low to Moderate Risk	80-100% Debt, 0-20% Equity, Equity-Oriented Investments
Moderate to High Risk	40-60% Debt, 40-60% Equity, Equity-Oriented, Alternate Investment
High Risk	0-20% Debt, 80-100% Equity, Equity-Oriented, Alternate Investment

(You may take an expert's help in assessing your risk appetite)

For a financial goal you need to look at the risk that you are willing to take to assess the expected returns, then provide for the savings needed. Practically this can be done through a historical return analysis or scenario analysis of investment options. Well, we have practical ways to balance risk – return without involving too much of a mathematical model. Do remember two aspects of the risk.

One, risk return balance is very specific to you, no two persons can have the same risk profile. And second, risk return balance would be specific to your financial goal too.

Approach # 1: Asset Allocation – As is prudently said about investments, don't put all your eggs in one basket. Put your investment across assets like equity, debt or alternates assets. These can be done directly by investing in these assets or indirectly though investment vehicles like mutual funds; ULIPs etc.

The fundamental aspect of asset allocation is to take the benefit of distinct risk – return profiles of the asset classes. For example, in an emerging market like India with a lower interest rate regime, equity markets normally do better or vice versa, with a combination of these two assets (Equity & Debt) you can balance risk. Similarly you can consider adding other assets like gold or real estate to balance risk.

The proportion of the asset in your portfolio depends on the horizon of a particular financial goal, liquidity requirements and your risk appetite. Let's illustrate this with the example of a sample asset allocation for an individual for his financial goals:

Goal	Equity	Debt	Cash	Weight
1	50%	40%	10%	20%
2	10%	60%	30%	20%
3	40%	60%	0%	20%
4	0%	50%	50%	20%
5	100%	0%	0%	20%
Total	40%	42%	38%	100%

Though a person could be younger in age, if his financial goals need an asset allocation as above, there is little scope of increasing asset allocation to equity. Though the general risk profile suggests that cash % should be much lesser and equity allocation should be higher.

As also for a financial goal you need to balance assets at regular intervals, from riskier investment at the beginning of the goal to safer assets so that at the time of realisation of the goal, market movements do not impact your financial goal and you get the proceeds with certainty.

Approach # 2: Diversification – Diversification is the key to risk management and it is the most fundamental principle of investments further within a particular asset class, also diversified by distributing funds. For example, if you are investing in an equity market, distribute funds across 4-5 sectors and within the sectors 2-3 stocks; one could be large cap, medium cap and third could be small cap stock. If you are investing in the equity markets through mutual funds, then you already have a diversified portfolio and you can further diversify by investing in different schemes of a mutual fund. For example, if it is a large cap fund in which you have invested than you can invest in small and mid-cap scheme.

Similar approach is needed for building debt and alternate investment portfolios. With different instruments in your diversified portfolio the effect of one instrument or security is then minimum, and the portfolio performance would be better compared to what it would have been without adequate diversification. While diversification will help you in managing the risk specific to a security or asset, you still carry market risk in that portfolio.

Approach # 3: Investment Cost Averaging – A technique to diversify your investment horizon, i.e., time diversification, this is also known as dollar cost averaging. In the financial market the simple principle to make money is to buy at low and sell at high so the difference is your profit; easier said than done, in the financial market this is the most difficult task. Even market experts would give up in timing the market.

The effective way is to invest in piecemeal over a longer horizon, this way you would be buying securities regularly. A fixed amount is invested to buy the securities over a period of time. When the market is low you get more units and when the market is high you get lesser units of the security. In a volatile market the average cost of buying units is lesser and to your advantage as the risk of investing lump sum at a wrong time is greatly reduced. In case, the market is following just one trend this could be disadvantageous for you. But in the long run it gives better results.

The concept is used in Systematic Investment Plans or SIPs and Systematic Transfer Plans or STPs offered by the mutual funds. SIPs can also be effectively done with direct stock investments wherein you buy stocks of selected companies for a fixed amount. Your stock broker should have stock SIP facility.

Approach # 4: Fixed Proportion Portfolio – This is another way to keep emotions and market timing away from growing a portfolio, when you have a lump sum amount to invest. In this technique you decide a fixed % for assets in a portfolio, which is updated regularly, say every quarter. Securities within the asset classes are sold and bought for the equivalent amount. For example, let's consider two asset portfolios of ₹ 10 lac with debt and equity and let's assume that both are kept in same proportion i.e. 50-50; ₹ 5 lac each in the debt and equity markets and the review period is a quarter. In both asset classes you buy securities which are liquid enough in the market for easy transactions. After a quarter, let's assume that the portfolio has grown to ₹ 10.6 lacs, out of which, equity has grown to ₹ 5.5 lacs and debt, ₹ 5.1 lac. To make it equal, you need to sell stocks for ₹ 0.2 lac and buy debt securities for the same amount. This way you would hold equity and debt at ₹ 5.3 lacs each. This process continues as long as you hold the portfolio. In between, you may decide to change the proportions based on your need or when goal achievement is approaching closer.

In a falling equity market, the stocks would be cheaper, so while balancing your portfolio, you should sell debt securities and buy stocks and accumulate them. In a growing market you ought to sell stocks to buy debt securities, thereby you can profit from the market movement and your portfolio will grow over a period of time.

Balanced Fund Schemes offered by the mutual funds work on a similar line. You can build your own portfolio with two or more assets in the beginning after carefully deciding on the proportion of these assets, and selecting securities carefully. The remaining task is to simply balance your portfolio at regular intervals.

The idea in managing risk–return balance is to make objective decisions rather than being swayed by emotions. Overexposing or taking higher risk is not prudent when it's not needed and at the same time not taking enough risk is said to be one of the biggest risks, the other one being not knowing what you are doing. Therefore to manage risk two things are important- one, take only appropriate risk and two, increase your knowledge of financial markets.

Concept # 2: Money Has Time Value

Money has time value. Let's understand this concept with an example; assume you have forgotten a ₹ 1000 currency note in a book and you get it back after a year while going through that book again. It is good that you got your money back, but would it be of the same value? Though the face value remains ₹ 1000, its actual value will be lower due to the rate of inflation, say lower by about 6-7% on an average. However, if this money had been invested, it would have fetched you some returns, say about 8-9%; this opportunity cost is the time value of money.

Your investment works on time value and you will appreciate the fact that an investment is both simple and complicated, it depends on how you take it. For long term investment it is easy to comprehend the investment mechanics. A simple formula will explain the nuances of investment and help in deciding on investment amount allocation. Let's get a little insight into investment mathematics with this little formula!

And the formula is **FAIREST**

"Here is the FAIREST formula to let money grow"

$$FA = Ix\,(1{+}R)^T$$

Future Amount = Investment × (1 + Rate of Return) ^{T}

FA - Future Amount available at the end of time period T and inclusive of initial investment made and interest thereon

I – Amount being invested now

R – Rate of return or interest rate on amount invested

T – Time for which investment is made

The aim of any investment is to maximise FA, i.e., Future Amount which in turn depends on three factors:

First is I (amount being invested now), which is the function of savings. Higher the savings higher would be the amount available for investment.

Second is R (rate of return on amount invested), which depends on underlying asset and in case of a portfolio of investment asset allocation which in turn depends on your risk appetite.

Third is T (time for which investment is made), which in financial planning parlance is the time available to complete the goal.

For maximising FA the simple task is to maximise:

1. "I" invest more and for investing more you need to save more, it is as simple as that.
2. Invest for a longer period i.e. higher "T" .

The formula can be rewritten as below for ease of mathematical calculation.

$$FA = I \times FVIFL$$

Notations are the same, FVIFL is the factor which is combination of "R" rate of return (or interest rate) and Time "T" for lump sum (i.e. one time) payment. FVIFL values can be tabulated, please refer to appendix VIII for FVIFL values.

This formula is applicable for lump sum or one time investment. For recurring investments where a fixed amount is invested at a regular interval the formula is:

$$FA = IA \times FVIFA$$

Notations are the same, FVIFA is the factor which is a combination of "R" rate of return (or interest rate) and Time "T" for fixed monthly amount. FVIFA values can be tabulated, please refer to appendix IX for FVIFA values.

Recall 'LIFE' (1. **L**ong Term, 2. **I**nvest Regularly, 3. **F**ixed Financial Goals and 4. **E**arly Start), these LIFE principles emphasise on this simple formula for reaping benefits of investments. In a quest to maximise FA, we often try to maximise R and invest in riskier assets. This investment eventually becomes out of alignment as far as risk is concerned. With a longer term in your hand you have better protection for risk and you have time to take corrective action too, should anything go against the selected financial goals.

Do not be afraid of looking at these formulas, these are handy and easy to use and you can work it out with a simple calculator on your mobile phone to see the value of your investment with the help of investment tables. This is useful in knowing the amount available in future. Let's work on a few illustrations:

Illustration # 1

You make **a lump sum deposit** of ₹ 1 lac today for 3 years in a company deposit at 10% p.a. compounded annually and the interest along with principal amount is payable on maturity. Let's see what you will get at the maturity:

FA = I x FVIFL

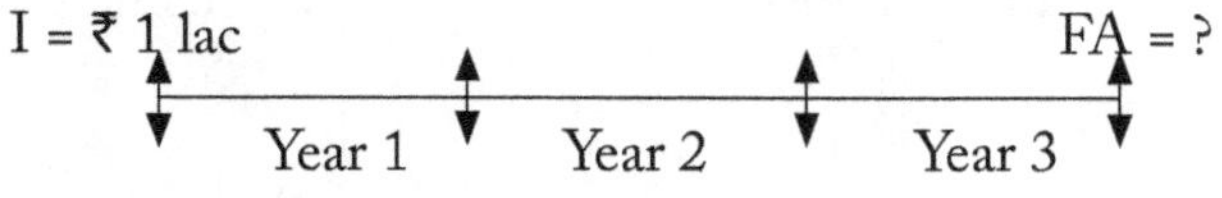

I = ₹ 1 lac FA = ?

Year 1 Year 2 Year 3

Here I = ₹ 1 lac

FVIFL for 10% p.a. and for 5 years in the table (Appendix IX) is 1.331

FA = ₹ 1 lac x 1.331

FA = ₹ 1.331 lac

Therefore on maturity you will get ₹ 1.331 lac

You make **a regular investment** of ₹ 1 lac every year for 3 years in a company deposit at 10% p.a. compounded annually and the interest along with the principal amount is payable on maturity. Let's see what you will get at the time of maturity:

FA = IA x FVIFA

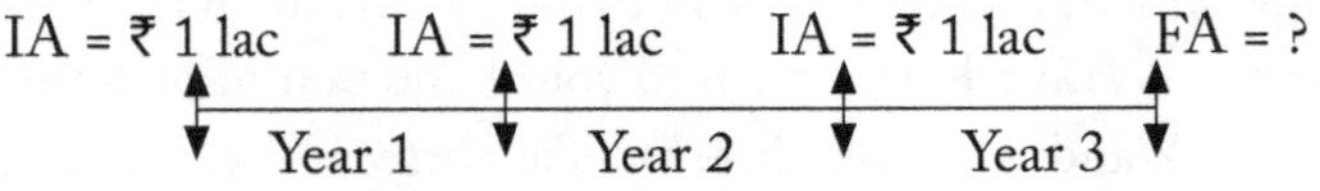

IA = ₹ 1 lac | IA = ₹ 1 lac | IA = ₹ 1 lac | FA = ?

Year 1 | Year 2 | Year 3

Here IA = ₹ 1 lac

FVIFA for 10% p.a. and for 5 years in the table (Appendix IX) is 3.31

FA = ₹ 1 lac x 3.31

FA = ₹ 3.31 lac

Therefore on maturity you will get ₹ 3.31 lac

You may have an amount receivable in future and want to see what actually it would be worth at that time. For example, you would receive a PF amount for ₹ 30 lacs at retirement which is due in 15 years. Let's see how much is it worth? These calculations are called present value calculations, using the same method with slight changes in the parameters (instead of F i.e. future we shall use P i.e. present)

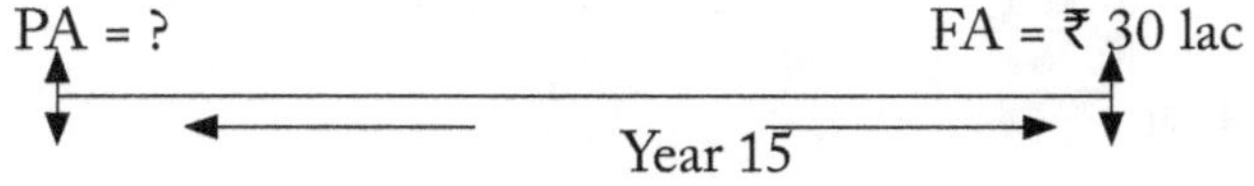

PA = ? | FA = ₹ 30 lac

Year 15

PA = I x PVIFL

PA - Present value of the Amount available at the end of time period T

PVIFL values can be taken from the table given in the appendix
Here I = ₹ 30 lac
PVIFL for 6% p.a., assumed average rate of inflation and for 15 years in the PVIFL table (Appendix IX) is 0.417

PA = ₹ 30 lac x 0.417
PA = ₹ 12.51 lac

Therefore the worth of the amount receivable at the end of 15 years would be ₹ 12.51 lac

Illustration # 4

Let's take an illustration where you have a financial product wherein you would get ₹ 1 lac at the end of every year for 5 years, let's assume rate of return is 8% p.a. with this rate of return let's see how much you would be willing to pay to buy this product?

In this case we shall use the formula,

PA = IA x PVIFA
Here I = ₹ 1 lac
PVIFA for 8% p.a. and for 5 years in the PVIFA table (Appendix IX) is 3.993

PA = ₹ 1 lac x 3.993
PA = ₹ 3.993 lac

Therefore the return from the investment has a worth of ₹ 3.993 lac, you can consider to invest if the above financial product is available at or below ₹ 3.993 lac.

Concept # 3: Borrowings Make Sense

In financial planning, when a financial goal is planned the aim is to achieve it by saving money and investing it to get the requisite amount on time. Borrowing comes into the picture on two occasions; first, when you are short of your targeted amount at the time when needed and second, when you have an opportunity to borrow for a particular financial goal, i.e., either borrowing is available at an attractive rate or it offers tax advantages to make effective cost lesser.

Out of these two, the first one is quite obvious, and you have no option but to resort to loan from the bank or from other sources like PF, personal loan etc. for fulfilling your financial goal. You can repay the loan in due course from savings. Consider the second scenario when you may not need the loan, however, you have an opportunity to avail a loan. There are certain areas where you get loans at attractive rates or rates become attractive because of the tax advantages; for example housing loan, education loan or personal loan from employer at an attractive rate of interest. In such cases, it may be a wise decision to avail the loan and the amount accumulated from investment is invested further. In the end, you can get better net returns.

Let's consider that you are buying a home with a budget of ₹ 50 lacs and have accumulated say ₹ 15 lacs, you had planned for ₹ 15 lacs margin and a loan of ₹ 35 lacs owing to your loan eligibility. Because of changes in your income you can now avail loan say up to ₹ 40 lacs. You have an option to avail loan for ₹ 40 lacs and add your margin of ₹ 10 lacs. With the interest rate on housing loans being competitive and tax advantages making it further cheaper, you have an opportunity to avail a full loan and from your corpus, invest ₹ 5 lacs to earn some returns or deploy this fund to your other planned financial goals.

Let's consider another example. You have provided for your kid's education, and at the time of funds requirement you decide to explore educational loans for your kid. The interest rate and term of the education loan is such that you think it is a wise decision to avail a loan and not break the investment for now. Also, you come to know that during the period of study you need to pay only interest and repayment may begin after completion of studies. This can be repaid by your kid after taking up a job. That sounds manageable, moreover tax advantages make the loan further attractive. You avail the loan and keep your money invested to earn returns or direct the funds to other financial goals or set another financial goal to say, accumulate wealth for your kid's marriage or for business capital.

The effective interest rate that you pay on the borrowing depends upon:

1. Actual borrowing rate
2. Compounding
3. Tax benefits, if any
4. Penal provisions like foreclosure charges, insurance cost, and late payment fee etc.

For example, if the interest rate on housing loan is say 10.5 % p.a. and you are in the 20% tax bracket the effective interest rate is 10.5% x (1-0.2) = 8.4%

Like it is advised to assess investment portfolio regularly, it is equally important to assess the loan portfolio too. And during assessment, the task should be to lower the interest cost. This can be done by exploring the possibility of discharging high interest rate loan by availing either low interest rate loan or from the investment which is earning or expected to earn lower returns. For example, if you have an outstanding credit card amount which is likely to be rolled over and in the next few months you will be paying part payment, then instead of paying high cost of interest pay this off by availing loan against property which is a cheaper loan or from some existing investment.

Likewise, if you have a housing loan and if you find a better loan offer, switch it. But first, do a cost-benefit analysis of switching loans to a different lending institution. Find out if you have to pay any additional charges in the process of switching loans. If you are privy to a loan at an attractive rate and if you can build a good portfolio, you can explore this opportunity too. However this should be done with full diligence with all the risks in mind. Never borrow money to speculate in the market.

While doing your financial planning, you should openly look out for a borrowing opportunity also but the following important points should be remembered:

1. Keep the source of possible borrowings to you handy.
2. Though it is obvious that you should avail loan from a lender who offers the least interest rate, be cautious about hidden fee and other charges, which can eventually increase the cost of borrowing.
3. Comprehend loan terms and conditions before signing the loan document. Normally, when a loan is availed these terms and conditions are overlooked.
4. Before borrowing, work on a repayment plan; you should not get trapped in the vicious circle of borrowing for retiring another loan. Unless you are consciously borrowing to reduce the borrowing cost by replacing a high cost loan which was not available earlier.
5. Do not fall into the trap of a limited period offer; do not decide in a hurry.
6. Keep your CIBIL record clean, pay every due on time.
7. Explore different lending institutions before you avail a loan, and negotiate interest rate before borrowing, do not forget you are a customer for them.
8. If you need borrowing, see which loan to avail for reducing the interest rate, if you need to borrow through personal loans, see if you can avail other loans like loan against house or property, the interest rate would be low if you could do that.
9. Keep loan portfolio up to date.
10. Get a loan pre-sanctioned if the need be, you will get better offers from other banks and lending institutions.

Concept # 4: Save Tax but not at any Cost

Tax planning is an essential element of financial planning. Taxation is a matter which infuriates everyone and there is always a curiosity about how to save on taxes. Within the tax framework you should minimise the tax, however you should see the opportunity cost too. Sometimes it is better to pay tax and invest the rest in a good investment product. There are instances when in order to save the tax we delay the decision. For example you are getting good capital appreciation on a stock but to get the entire capital gain exempt from the tax you need to hold for a year. In the quest of tax saving if you hold it for that period, it is quite possible that the price may not stay at the same level that is prevailing today, therefore instead of aiming at tax savings, maximise post-tax return by paying taxes or with tax management.

In the financial planning realm, an advisor would suggest you to not just look at the tax work in accordance with overall financial goal, but that tax planning should be a part of it. With this conscious approach towards tax planning all your asset allocation would remain intact, otherwise due to an impulsive decision to save taxes, your risk profile, asset allocation and final goals will all get distracted.

During the financial planning process, select investment products which save tax for you as well. The motto of financial planning is very simple and it is captured in the sentence "everything is planned"; there are several ways in which you can effectively plan tax savings and achieve your financial goal by keeping both in alignment with each other.

For example, if you buy protection for your family the premium paid qualifies for the section 80C benefit; with protection planning your tax planning is partly taken care of. For example, if you are allocating funds for equity for a long term investment and you want to save too, you can consider ELSS of mutual funds, which will give you the double benefits of equity exposure and tax savings. Similarly, you can plan tax savings with borrowings too, like home loans, education loans come with tax advantages associated with it. Tax planning is specific to your profession and also specific to your sources of income.

For better tax planning, if you look at the nature and source of your income and expenses, barring general household expenses, you shall find some opportunity to save tax. For example, if it is a house loan then interest payment and principal repayment as well stamp duty offer tax benefits under different heads of taxations as per IT act. Similarly, medical expenses including medical insurance, tuition fee of the kids, interest payment on education loan, donations, rent paid, HRA etc. If expense heads like these are analysed you will find some way of saving tax too.

Like tax benefits available to an individual, you can create an entity which will be eligible for tax benefits. The entity that you can create is the Hindu Undivided Family or HUF as it is popularly known. An HUF is considered to be a separate legal entity under the Income Tax Act. It arises by birth and not by mere agreement between family members. Individuals who are covered by Hindu law can form HUF. In addition to a Hindu, Sikh, Buddhist and Jain family can form an HUF. From the income tax point of view an HUF is a separate entity. Let's take two general illustrations to understand the tax benefits of HUF:

Illustration #1: Assume that a member governed by the Hindu law starts a business; in addition to income from salary he would have income from business too. Tax savings when he forms an HUF and does business in HUF is quite substantial compared to when he does business on his own.

S.No.	Income Particulars	Scenario I	Scenario I		Remarks
		Individual Assessment	Individual Tax Assessment	HUF Tax Assessment	
1	Salary	850000	850000	-	Income from salary
2	Business Income	700000	-	700000	Income from business

3	Gross Total Income	1550000	850000	700000	Total of income from income heads
4	Deductions u/s 80C	150000	150000	150000	Sec 80C benefits available to individuals and HUF both
5	Net Taxable Income	1400000	700000	550000	Net taxable income is divided in individual and HUF, benefit of lower slab rate
6	Tax Liability	239475	54075	23175	Net saving of ₹ 162225

Illustration # 2: Assume that a member governed by the Hindu law has income from salary and rental income from ancestral property. Again tax savings when he forms an HUF and transfers ancestral property to the HUF is quite substantial compared to the opposing scenario.

S.No.	Income Particulars	Scenario I	Scenario I		Remarks
		Individual Assessment	Individual Tax Assessment	HUF Tax Assessment	
1	Salary	1000000	1000000	-	Income from salary
2	Rental Income	500000	-	500000	Income from rent
3	Gross Total Income	1500000	1000000	500000	Total of income from income heads
4	Deductions u/s 80C	150000	150000	150000	Sec 80C benefits available to individual and HUF both
5	Net Taxable Income	1350000	850000	350000	Net taxable income is divided in individual and HUF, benefit of lower slab rate
6	Tax Liability	224025	84975	5000	Net saving of ₹ 134050

In both the above illustrations, more than calculations it is important to comprehend that with an additional tax entity in the form of HUF you could save quite substantially on tax owing to available deductions u/s 80C and benefit of lower marginal tax rate which otherwise would have been taxed at a higher marginal rate. Therefore, in general, additional income other than salary can be created in this new entity i.e. HUF.

Once an HUF is created it has its own sources of income which is taxed separately, own assets and liabilities as a separate entity. An HUF can invest in tax saving instruments like an individual; it can invest in mutual funds, stocks and can take insurance policy of its members. An HUF can own a business; can be partner in a business. An HUF can buy property and avail housing loan thereby getting the tax advantage on housing loan interest payment too. The HUF can be created by the head of the family, and he acts as *Karta* of the HUF. His wife, his children & their family can be members of the HUF. The *Karta* manages affairs on behalf of the HUF.

When you decide to create an HUF and have requisite family members, then apply for a PAN card for the HUF, complete a few formalities, open a bank account and transfer inherited assets, assets which are generating tax free income, seek gifts etc. to begin generating income. As you have seen in the illustrations, an HUF enjoys tax exemptions and marginal tax rates as an individual assessee. Like other provisions of the income tax laws with the creation of an HUF you can save substantial tax well within the tax framework. With so many benefits of an HUF if you have not created one, the time is now!

Concept # 5: Take care of Family and Dependents with Estate Planning

There are certain important issues which often get neglected and are sometimes considered mere formalities, which however ought to be completed and proactively pursued to make your financial plan complete. Estate planning is one such important issue. With every investment and scheme where there would be someone of your family benefiting or for whose benefit you have entered into a transaction, you need to make your intention clear with strong affirmation. In general most of the things are presumed and also normally your investment advisor or banker may not openly talk about beneficiary or beneficiaries, so you have to make it very clear who your intended beneficiaries are. What looks very obvious may not really be so, therefore it is better to keep it clear and make it clear to those who matter, so that money is received and used by those who were intended to receive the money.

Broadly, there are three ways to make your financial transactions with clear intention as to who is going to benefit in your absence, these are nomination, trust, and will. Fourth could be Power of Attorney i.e. POA which has a very specific or just transaction oriented use, therefore it is not considered here for a detailed discussion.

1. Nomination – Choosing a nominee may not be mandatory in some cases but it is a must for prudent financial planning and should not be postponed. Whenever you fill a form for an investment, Demat account, bank account, insurance or any other transaction where "nomination field" appears, do complete it too. A nominee is a person who is entitled to receive the funds and proceeds in the unfortunate event that the original investor is deceased. A nominee may or may not be entitled to consume the proceeds, which depends on the will or legal status of the nominee. With a nominee to assume responsibilities, proceeds will be made available quicker with some formalities and can be passed to the beneficiaries quickly and without any hassles. In the absence of a nominee more formalities would be needed, and legal heirs would then need to authenticate themselves before the proceeds are made available to them.

It is possible to nominate more than one person with the percentage of portion that they may receive in case such a need arises. A trust can also be nominated, however you may need to check the investment specifically to see if they allow only individuals or trusts also. You may change the nomination at any time and also any number of times. It also happens during the start of the career your parents could be the nominee, later, with the family, your spouse could also become a nominee and as the family expands kids can become nominees too.

This is a very simple step but it goes a long way in securing the future of your loved ones for whom the financial planning is undertaken. Therefore, without any hesitation you should have a nominee or nominees for every investment account wherever you have a nomination field. If it is pending for any of your investments or accounts you must do it now.

2. Will – It is again a very sensitive as well as sensible issue. A will is your will written to benefit all those you really intend to benefit after you. In the absence of a will, respective personal law would precede and the asset would be distributed in accordance with that. So what is obvious may not be the case if it is not written and may lead to disputes.

A will is a very simple document stating your will to whom your assets should go after you. Any person irrespective of quantum of wealth can write his or her will and you should write a will irrespective of your wealth. A will can be hand written or typed and may or not be registered. However it is better to be registered so there are minimum legal disputes, if any do arise. A will is a very personal document to you, it need not be shown to any one, except when it is needed. It need not to be shown to the witnesses, they are the witness to your signing the will. In no way does a will interfere with your assets or affect your ownership of the assets. You may freely transact as you could do in the absence of a will.

While writing a will make it clear that it is not being made under any influence or pressure, it must be dated with your correct name and address. The will which is the latest, in case there are more than one wills, will be enforceable superseding all previous wills. Appoint a trustworthy person in the will as an executor to execute it. Keep the will as simple as possible with very clear instructions with regard to each of the assets, with due details to avoid any confusion or wrong interpretation. It should clearly talk about who will get which asset and when. Make the will clear to that extent.

It is recommended though not necessary to take the services of a legal advisor in the process. A will is something which must be created by everyone, if you have not done it yet, the right time is now!

3. Trust – A trust is created for the benefit of the intended beneficiary or beneficiaries. The trusts we are talking about are private trusts for the benefit of family members, particularly kids. A trust can be created, for example, for your kids for taking care of their education expenses and post education marriage expense till they attain a certain age. After initial contribution towards a trust so created, the trust will invest, receive the income and provide for expenses or accumulate funds for the intended benefits. This adds to the certainty and very clearly benefits the beneficiaries.

In forming a trust there are three parties to it, one who creates a trust, one who manages the affairs of the trust and the third is the beneficiary who will eventually get the wealth of the trust. When you create a trust, which is a legal entity, you are the 'trustor' or 'settler' who establishes the trust guidelines in the trust deed which gets registered, appoint trustees and set how the beneficiaries will be benefited. The trust gets its assets when you transfer funds or assets to the trust which is then managed by the trustees for the benefit of intended beneficiaries. Assets once transferred to the trust may or may not be possible to be received back by you. Investment and income generated by the trust may or may not save tax for you. A trust so created is not for tax planning but is essentially an 'estate planning' mechanism to benefit the intended beneficiaries.

As a parent you may create a trust to take care of your kids' future, it is all the more necessary if some special care is needed, this way the future of the kids will be secured. With the trust any family dispute, property dispute or business failure's impact on family will not hamper the trust's wealth, hence beneficiaries' futures will be safe and secure to that extent. From an estate planning point of view, with the trust you have added benefits of control over your assets and the trust deed can specify who should distribute the assets to whom and when. So, when assets are distributed to the beneficiaries, it can remain free from creditors and other heirs who are not intended to be the beneficiaries. Also, in cases where a beneficiary is a minor, transfer of assets may lead to some difficulties on how the assets will be managed but a trust could be a solution in such cases.

Creation of trust and writing a will both are aimed at well-defined estate planning or succession planning. In a trust, asset transfers happen in your presence whereas in a will it happens posthumously. You can ensure that the trust is running smoothly for intended benefits. Trust remains a private affair and there is no probate whereas a will may become public. In a trust the beneficiary is known to those concerned and it may be contested in the family, if that may be the case in case: of will it need not be disclosed. In a trust you may or may not lose control of your property to the trust created by you, while in a will it is just writing and no transfer happens till the end. This is not however a choice issue, you can create both a trust and write a will. The essence is to have clear estate planning in place to ensure smooth handover of your wealth to the hands of the beneficiary whom you wanted to be the benefactor.

Concept # 6: Keep Updating Financial Knowledge

In the world of finance a little investment of time could be handsomely rewarding. You should be ready to take the benefit of opportunities offered by the financial markets or government schemes. This can be done if you keep yourself updated with the market developments and are equipped with the fundamentals of finance to comprehend what is happening in the financial market place and how it impacts your portfolio. It is not at all about market timing or predicting the market to get enticed by short term market movements, it is about looking around for structural changes that might be impacting your portfolio. There are ways though in which you can increase your financial knowledge and be able to take informed decisions and be able to question and debate with your financial advisor.

1. Read, Read and Read - There are several sources to gather information, whichever suits you adopt one or two.

A. Business Newspapers – This investment which is not more than ₹ 500 per month will keep you updated with what's happening in the business world. Most of the business dailies run pages on personal finance which will help you further to compare your financial plan.

B. Business Magazines – Business magazines on personal finance will keep providing you with updated information relevant to you. Keep enriching yourself with these magazines.

C. Web Posts – There are so many websites which carry information on personal finance. You can gather good knowledge from websites of your financial advisory firms. Select two to three websites with which you are comfortable.

D. Books – Read books on investment, financial markets and personal finance. There are good books which are full of insights and could prove to be your guide in the financial planning process.

2. Meet People – Meeting financial experts helps in getting valuable insights. Do meet investment advisors and learn about new products; meet subject matter experts occasionally to discuss your queries. You need not buy something whenever you meet someone.

3. Attend Seminars – Attend investor awareness camps organised by regulatory authorities, investment institutions and by local clubs. You will learn new aspects about your finances. Your banker or investment advisor can help you in informing about such events. Financial institutions also run training programs for consumers, which are extremely good in content and you would enjoy learning. Experience it!

4. Technology - IT can help you a lot in gathering relevant information when needed. There are mobile applications on investment and personal finance. Create web alerts for news that you want and subscribe to free newsletters. You can join one or two relevant web forums or groups which will keep sharing information, and you can follow one or two good blogs which post regular updates.

5. Join a course – You may join a short course, a distance learning course or an online course on personal finance. There are courses which are very cost effective and extremely good in content. Try one or two short courses on equity markets, mutual funds etc. to gain some insights.

6. Television – This is the handiest tool to keep yourself updated if the TV is allowed to stay on the business news channel. Watching a couple of high quality general business programs for an hour everyday should suffice.

You may read newspapers, magazines, blogs, mail alerts etc. at your will but do read them. You need not follow every piece of advice but it will help you in taking informed decisions.

Develop your way to gather information and with some practice it will become a habit and after a few day of this rewarding habit, you will need a few minutes to know the things that you have set for yourself and do keep revising the way you gather the information

It pays to know more; as said by Benjamin Franklin, "An investment in knowledge pays the best interest."

7. Plan Your Own Goal: Amazingly Achievable

"Let our advance worrying become advance thinking and planning"
- Winston Churchill

Financial goals are unique to an individual, which are too significant to an individual and the family. What's a financial goal? Before that, what's a goal? A goal could be a dream or necessity for the self or for the family. A goal could be buying a house. Based on background and circumstances it could be a 1BHK flat or 2BHK flat or a bigger flat, or it could be a bungalow or for some it could be a second home or it could be a farmhouse or the like. A financial goal is a goal which is realistic and time bound, which is determined by you based on your aspirations and circumstances like present level of income and future growth in income, accumulated wealth, financial help from the family, inheritance etc. So while a goal could be buying a house, a financial goal would be to buy a 3 BHK flat in 3 years' time from now.

Once a financial goal is decided, the next immediate step is to see the funds flow needed. There could be three possible ways or combinations of these ways in which funds will be needed to achieve planned financial goals:

1. Initial lump sum payment

2. Regular payment during the tenure of the financial goal

3. Lump sum payment on achieving the goal

Please remember we are analszing the nature of funds needed to achieve the financial goal and not the financing aspects of it. For example, for buying a house if you need ₹ 75 lac. For the seller the need is initial lump sum payment, only then the ownership will be transferred to you. Another example is planning for your kid's marriage, the amount so needed is mostly the lump sum payment at the time of achieving the goal. In retirement planning funds are needed during the tenure, i.e., post retirement period. Planning for education for kids would be a combination of regular payment and lump sum payments.

The idea for analysing funds flow is to arrange for funds when needed and deciding on asset allocation too.

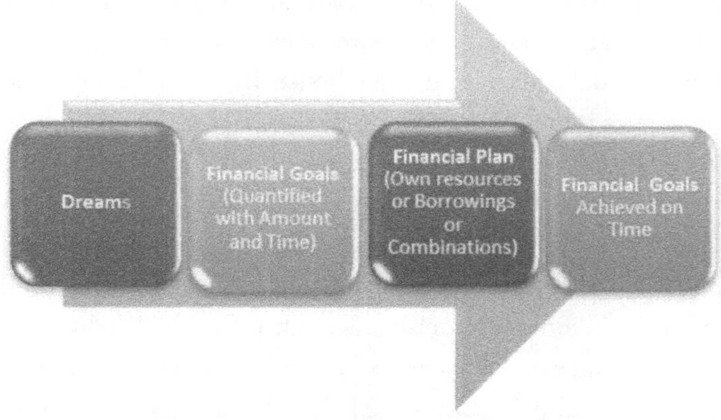

Illustrations 7.1: Arranging for funds to turn dreams into reality

There could be three ways to finance planned financial goals:

1. Funding from accumulated resources
2. Funding through systematic regular savings
3. Borrowing

In most of the cases, it is a combination of all the three sources for funding financial goals. Which of the sources are to be used and in what proportion all depends on the quantum of funds needed and on the cost of funding. The cost is interest rate or opportunity cost of savings. It would be a task of channelising the existing savings for the financial goal if you have enough resources to deploy, however there would still be scope of maximising return if borrowings is resorted to. In most of the cases a corpus is built through systematic investing and it is quite common too, to start with smaller savings to build a bigger corpus. Do follow LIFE principles.

In case of borrowings, there could be specific schemes with the bank or lending institutions to fund your financial goals, for example a housing loan or an education loan. The benefit of availing finance in such cases is lower interest rate and longer repayment period, which gives you flexibility to plan repayment period. Otherwise, interest cost would be higher. There could be several ways to borrow depending upon your professional status. This could be loan from PF account, borrowing against fixed deposit or NSC, personal loan, gold loan, loan against property etc.

Let's work out a few financial goals. For giving proper order and due importance let's regroup the financial plan:

A. Planning for Protection
    1. Provide for emergency
    2. Protection for assets, healthcare & living standard
B. Planning for High Priority Goals
    1. Children's education
    2. Children's marriage
C. Retirement Planning
D. Other Planning
    1. Estate planning
    2. Philanthropic activities

E. Wealth Creation

"Plan for our
LIFE goals now"

The list indicates common financial goals and can surely be extended for one's need, present life stage and level of preparation.

You should create your own list of financial goals. The goals could be retiring debt, accumulating for parents, sponsoring a family event etc. specific to your customs and culture. The goal could also be accumulating a corpus for starting a business for self or for the spouse, something specific to their own inspirations.

Let's begin the task.

I. Planning for Protection

1. Providing for an Emergency i.e. creating a corpus for meeting exigencies which may require immediate cash. Let's work this out first -

What is an emergency? It is something which is unforeseen or unplanned. Since this may happen it is better that one prepares for it financially.

How much to keep aside for emergency? This depends on the nature of expenses one has and the kind of occupation one is involved in. However 3 to 6 times of monthly expenses need to be kept aside for meeting unplanned & unforeseen expenses. This amount should not be used for paying a loan instalment, paying credit card dues, buying household items etc. It is to be kept only for emergency and once any amount is used try and replenish that as early as possible to keep oneself prepared.

How is it to be done? A separate joint account can be opened to save targeted emergency funds. If you are familiar with net banking, managing online transactions would be easier.

Keeping entire money in savings account is not advisable as return would be too low and there are other options which can get you the benefit of liquidity provided you are comfortable investing in other effective options.

1. Liquid funds offered by asset management companies (mutual funds)
2. Combination of savings and fixed deposits accounts in a nearest bank.

There could be other avenues to park money for emergency funding, but that may not be as liquid as it is needed in case of emergency and secondly may be subjected to market fluctuations so you may not be certain about the amount you may get on liquidating such investments. Here, the question is not of total assets or investments that you have but the issue is liquidity of funds.

To quantify, let's assume that your gross income is ₹ 50000 per month, take home salary after statutory deductions & TDS is ₹ 40000 per month and monthly expenses including rent, household expenses, school fee etc. is ₹ 30000. If you decide to provide for 3 months emergency funding you need to provide for ₹ 30000 x 3 = ₹ 90000. This corpus can be built gradually or can be aligned from other existing investment gradually. The exact size of the emergency fund depends on a few important factors like:

1. Income Predictability – Higher the income predictability, lesser could be the size of the fund. For a salaried person whose income is fixed every month, a smaller corpus may work compared to a person whose monthly income is not fixed; there could be other income sources which will determine size of the emergency fund.

2. Level of household income – Fund size should be in proportion to monthly household income.Slightly higher in proportion for higher monthly household expenses, also higher where amount of non-discretionary expenses is high compared to discretionary expenses like leisure expenses

3. In addition other factors like existing protection covers (medical, household) ongoing loan or outstanding liabilities will determine the size of the emergency funds.

The benefits of developing emergency funding are:

I. Availability of funds as and when needed to meet an emergency, so you are better prepared.

II. Since it is planned, the funding will not be impacting other goals and your finances.

Just try and imagine the confidence you would have once you have provided yourself & your family with funds to meet any emergency, at least financially!

In terms of cost, creating emergency fund does not cost anything. However, opportunity cost of investment would be there. Since it is liquid assets, it would be a low return generating investment.

2. Protection for Assets, Healthcare & Living standards – One needs to look at protecting three broad issues financially,
A. Protection of assets
B. Protection of healthcare cost
C. Protection of living standards

Let's work on these three areas one-by-one:

A. Protection of Assets – Assets are acquired with hard-earned money and so have an emotional value too and assets which have been acquired can be protected by insuring those assets.

Assets that one can look at insuring are:-
1. House
2. Household items
3. Vehicle
4. Other valuables

Insurance is a mechanism of transferring risk but it comes at a price, therefore at times someone may decide to retain risk partly or fully. Since it comes at a price (called insurance premium) one needs to find an insurance cover which provides adequate coverage at the lowest cost possible.

Insurance cover or policy for assets are offered by general insurance companies (please refer to the appendix for a list of general insurance companies in India). You can seek help of an advisor or visit the website or nearest branch of any of the companies to get quotations for your requirement of protection of assets. Compare the quotation and finalise the insurance policy for your need. You may look at different covers for different assets if it is cost effective. Do look at claim handling & general services level and convenience before finalising a policy.

Once a policy is taken, keep it in safe custody and do renew on time. Also look at and create a record of insurance which is clubbed in acquiring assets. For example, while availing a home loan, house insurance is clubbed by the loan provider. While buying if there are guarantees associated keep a record of the same.

The cost is the total of annual premium that you have to pay.

B. Protection of Healthcare Costs

Health insurance is a must for everyone. No one would like to compromise when it comes to medical care for self and family members, in such an eventuality, by not protecting or by under protection of healthcare there would be a big dent on existing financials. Medical science is progressing day by day and so is the healthcare cost going up.

Health insurance cover (also called medical insurance) is the solution to protect against healthcare costs. It provides cover to meet expenses during hospitalisation and other medical expenses.

When you buy medical insurance you look at the amount of cover which is normally in the range of ₹.1 lac to ₹. 5 lac. This can be much higher too depending on one's need. The amount available in the cover is valid for a year, i.e., medical expenses admissible as claim under the policy can be reimbursed up to specified cover. A policy with says ₹ 3 lac cover entitles the policy holder to claim up to ₹ 3 lac during the year, subject to the claim being admissible as per policy terms.

Companies which provide medical insurance can be categorised:

1. General insurance companies
2. Health insurance companies
3. Life insurance companies which provide health insurance

(Refer to the appendix for the names of these companies)

Medical policies with various features and variants are offered by these companies. While selecting a medical policy one needs to look at:

1. Network of hospitals affiliated
2. Maximum age up to which it can be renewed
3. Premium for given cover
4. Policy features viz. floater cover, cashless claim settlement, service level
5. Policy constraints viz sub limits, pre post coverage, exclusions

There are certain policies which offer specialised medical covers viz. top up covers for higher medical cover once basic medical policy is taken, policy for critical illness etc, these policies can be considered based on one's need. One can also consider separate policies for elderly family members; it would be cost effective and policy renewal would be better manageable.

Family floater policy is commonly available and offers flexibility in sum assured. Floater indicates sum assured is available to all covered in the policy.

Selection of sum assured depends on:

1. Size of the family
2. Age of the family members being covered, particularly eldest member
3. Income
4. Individual cover and family cover
5. Top up option available

Once the assessment for desired health insurance cover is decided, one can select a suitable policy or combination of policies.

If you decide to top up cover further, one can take top up policy, by paying premium. There are variants available in medical insurance policies; you can select the plan & options best suited to your family.

The total premium paid towards medical insurance is the cost of medical insurance payable annually.

For a salaried individual, some of the employers also provide medical cover, in such a case it is essential to judge adequacy of cover and continuity of cover. If there is possibility of job change also in such cases it is suggested to take a separate policy to remain covered.

Once a medical policy is taken it should be kept in safe custody and timely renewal must be ensured to enjoy continued benefits. With the portability one can change the insurer on his choice.

Prevention is always better than cure. Having planned and provided for unforeseen medical exigencies it is advisable to take care of own health by checking one's diet and also deciding on a medical checkup plan for everyone in the family.

C. Protection of Living Standards

By following up on creating corpus for emergency funding and protecting family from health-care costs, one has planned substantially and planned for any eventuality in the presence of breadwinner. Protection of family standard is the amount needed today in case something unfortunate happens to the breadwinner (earning member) and this corpus would be immediately needed for survivors.

This requires calculations, which are slightly tedious due to the need to incorporate 1. present expenses 2. inflation and 3. expected return on investment, to estimate amount of corpus needed to maintain the same living standard adjusted for a. existing liabilities, and b. existing assets

Let's calculate, and to make the calculation simple we'll use the "Standard Table, Table No. 2" of "Financial Planning Easy Tables" given in Appendix – VIII.

Step 1: Estimate of monthly expenses, as worked in the budgeting exercise (Table 4 - Chapter - 4) monthly expenses including household expenses, education expenses etc. but excluding EMIs, insurance premium etc. are not difficult to estimate (more accurate calculation would involve year-by-year monthly expenses adjusted for inflation). Assume that monthly expenses for simplicity and ease of understanding are ₹ 25000 per month.

Step 2: Estimate the time period for which these monthly expenses would continue, for simplicity a thumb rule can be taken as:

Time period for expense provision, in years = (80 – Age of the bread winner)

This is an empirical formula; detailed study needs to be done to establish applicability for an individual. However for simplicity it is an easy approximation.

Assume age of the bread winner is 45 years, therefore

Time period for expense provision = (80 - 45) = 35 years

Step 3: Estimate corpus needed before adjusting for existing assets or liabilities

Amount of corpus needed = monthly expenses adjusted for inflation x number of years

In this illustration,

Amount needed = ₹ 25000 per month adjusted for inflation x 35 years

Refer value in Table 2 against 35 years, which is ₹ 2,23,975, this is the amount needed to get ₹ 1000 per month adjusted for inflation @6% p.a. and return on investment @10% p.a.

For ₹ 25000 per month amount needed is 25 x 223975 = ₹ 55,99,384 or approximately ₹ 56 lac

Step 4: Adjustment for outstanding liabilities & Assets

Assume that outstanding car loan is ₹ 3 lac and outstanding home loan is ₹ 20 lac. Further assuming that existing insurance cover is ₹ 10 lac, current valuation of investments ₹ 5 lac which is not marked for any financial goal. (Also assuming that other financial goals are adequately protected, if not that needs to be included in outstanding liabilities)

Amount of corpus needed

= Amount for monthly expenses (Amount in Step 3) to be provided + Outstanding Liabilities to be provided for - Existing Assets which can be used

= ₹ 56 lac
+ ₹ 3 lac car loan + ₹ 20 Lac home loan
– ₹ 10 lac insurance – ₹ 5 lac

= ₹ 64 lac

Step 5: Providing for the corpus – by buying life insurance cover for ₹ 64 lac. This is the life insurance cover needed immediately. This is an indicative simplistic calculation to estimate corpus needed immediately if something unfortunate happens to the sole earning member in the family.

With this corpus invested to earn a post-tax return of 10% p.a. would yield ₹ 25000 per month equivalent to adjust for inflation amount for next 35 years. i.e. in year 1 amount receivable would be ₹ 25,000 per month, in year 2 ₹ 26,500 per month, in year 3 ₹ 28,000 per month and so, in year 35, it would be ₹ 1,81,275 per month.

A host of life insurance products are available to fulfil this requirement. For pure risk, term plan (either online or from an advisor) will be able to meet this requirement.

Protection is a critical and essential part of financial planning. It is critical because without this, even good financial planning may get derailed and it is essential because it can de-risk financial goals and keep financial goal planning complete.

The cost of protection, therefore, is sum of premium paid towards taking insurance cover on assets, health cover & life insurance cover assuming it is a pure term cover.

The overall cost of protection including emergency funding is the sum of:

1. Opportunity cost of creating and maintaining emergency fund
2. Premium paid towards taking insurance cover on assets
3. Premium paid towards health and on health cover
4. Premium paid towards buying life insurance cover

This is a cost, regular cost by such time protection continues and yields no return on investment, however, there is no expectation of returns either. However incurring cost has intangible and tangible benefits. The level of assurances, confidence and peace of mind one would have cannot be quantified. This would ensure that subsequent financial goals including wealth creation would now be fructified, and in case of any eventuality, protection plan would come into play and will not put the family in financial difficulties and other financial goals will also not get affected.

II. Planning for High Priority Goals

We have different priorities in life; accordingly planning for high priority goals would take precedence over other financial goals. Here I am suggesting a few common high priority goals for the benefit of the readers:

1. Children's education
2. Children's marriage

These are high priority goals and given every chance parents would like to do their best. Financial planning can support in a big way in achieving financial goals for kids. The financial goals, which are taken here for illustration purposes are education and marriage. Difference between education and marriage as financial goals is in nature of funds required.

For education, funds are required regularly and in lump sum intermittently. For example for schooling up to 12th standard (junior college education) school fee, coaching expenses, books, school activities, uniform, PC, educational software etc. are regular in nature. During the college studies for graduation or postgraduation in addition to regular funds to cover routine college fee may need to pay in lump sum. Some parents may like to add funds for convenience and lifestyle too like buying electronic gadgets, mobile phones, motorbike or car etc. To summarise, it is regular funds requirements coupled with intermittent lump sum payment till the time their education is complete. Knowing this pattern is helpful in arranging for adequate funds with certainty.

Providing for education from monthly expenses bill, like household expenses is not a prudent strategy, because it dilutes planning for your kid's education. If parents plan for quality education for their child and start setting aside an amount, regularly or in lump sum or in combination, this will result in achievement of one of the most important milestones in a child's life comfortably and pleasantly.

Let's take a simple example, your child is 6 years today and 15 years from now you have to plan for postgraduate education in India or abroad and total one-time expenses are around 10 lac, if admission is sought today.

In 15 years' time the costs would go up due to inflation and therefore you need to plan for ₹ 10 lac adjusted for inflation. Assuming inflation of 6% p.a. the amount needed at the time of admission in PG program is approximately ₹ 24 lac. (Please refer "Inflation table, table 1, in appendix VIII, price of ₹ 1000 would become ₹ 2,397 in 15 years, 10 lac therefore would become 23.97 lac ~ ₹ 24 lac) You need to provide for ₹ 24 lac, hence planning would be done to accumulate ₹ 24 lac.

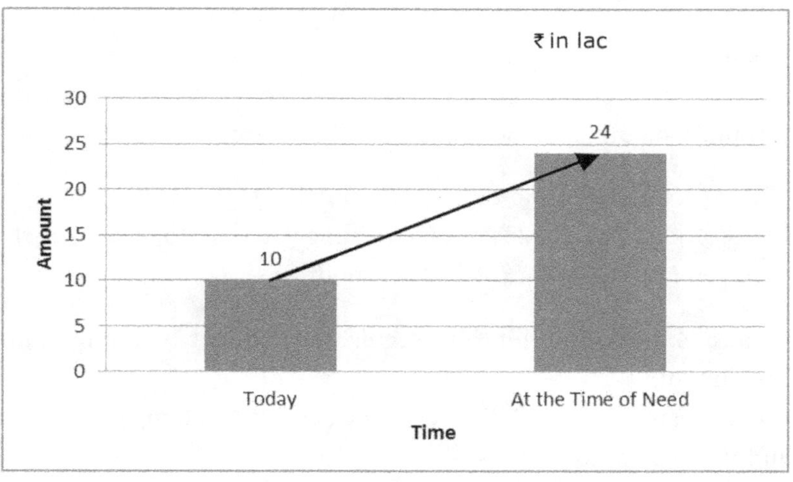

Illustration 7.2: Inflation impacts targeted amount

With planning, in due time you would ensure that requisite sum is available. Delay in planning will not stop price to rise i.e. you will still need ₹ 24 lac whether you plan or not. Only difference would be that with planning you would be able to provide for expenses, in absence of that, you will be needed to go for an option which is less expensive than this. It means lack of planning will lead to compromising on education for your child. This is a much heavier cost one would pay, by not planning, for their kids and compromising on education.

How this sum can be made available at the time of need:

Target Corpus = ₹ 24 lac
Available time = 15 years

Choice 1 – Monthly Regular Investment

Amount to be invested every month for 15 years assuming return on investment @10% p.a.
= ₹ 6,300 (approximately)

If you start now, by investing regular sum of ₹ 6,300 per month for 15 years will get you ₹ 24 lac.

Choice 2 – One Time Investment (Lump sum)
Instead of regular investment you want to set aside lump sum amount today, then amount needed is ₹ 5.75 lac

Choice 3 – Fixed Lump Sum + Monthly Regular Investment
Or assume you have ₹ 2 lac and remaining you want to save regularly then you need to invest ₹ 4,100 per month

Choice 4 – Fixed Monthly Regular Investment + Lump Sum Investment
Or you want to save ₹ 3,000 per month and rest in lump sum today, and then you need to invest ₹ 3 lac today

Choice 5 – Borrowing
Another option is borrowing, when funds are not sufficient and can be paid back by earning later. This could also be part of planning, however, at the time of applying for loan, the banker would decide on eligibility and amount of loan, therefore, one needs to keep track of loan eligibility for the amount of education loan needed. The loan repayment commences post completion of education. It offers tax benefits also.

What looked like a mammoth task becomes easily doable. Planning makes it simple and achievable. At the cost of repetition, planning early always helps. In choice 2, just to evaluate power of early planning, if time available would have been 20 years, i.e. for the same education planning would have started 5 years early (i.e. when the kid is just 1 year, though it is too early to decide about a career though it is not early to target a program and start planning towards that. Career option may change later but time cannot be recovered) the amount needed at that time was just ₹ 3.6 lac or Choice 3 would have needed ₹ 1 lac lump sum & ₹ 2,500 per month investment.

Consideration in Financial Planning for Kids' Education:

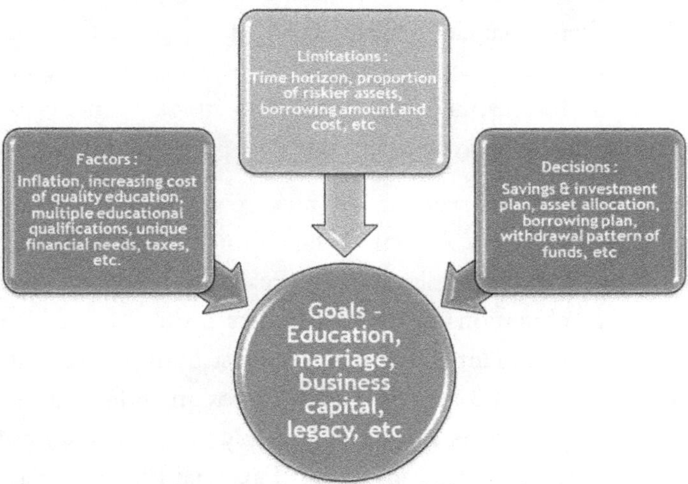

Illustration 7.3: Financial Planning for Kids' Education

1. Expenses Head – School fee, hostel or accommodation, books, coaching, library subscription, project expenses etc.

Identifying expense heads will help in better estimation and therefore in planning. However in the early stage it may be quite difficult to identify heads of expenses. In a majority of the cases it would be difficult to firm up career choice, which evolves over a period of time. In such cases, conservative lump sum expenses can be targeted and planning can be done without losing on time.

2. Time available for planning – More time will help in better planning and much lesser amount would be needed for targeted sum of amount. "LIFE" principles work better with availability of more time

3. Withdrawal pattern – The amount needed could be one time or distributed over a period of education. The fees, for example, could be one-time or every year over a period of educational program. The planning needs to be changed slightly to provide for funds distributed over a period of time.

4. Borrowing – Borrowing is also an option for funding educational expenses. This should also be part of planning. Educational institutes facilitate loans from financial institutions. If it is part of the plan, you need to keep yourself updated on eligibility, interest rate, and repayment terms for planned amount. There are tax benefits on interest component on repayment of loan.

For simplicity, for various scenarios of fund requirements, amount needed are tabulated below. Amount is taken for ₹ 1 lac to facilitate easy estimation for different amount, approximate amount. There could be more combinations for ease of understanding, a few have been indicated. For amount more than 1 lac just multiply requisite amount in lac to column 3 and column 4. For example for ₹ 5 lacs targeted amount in 10 years in case 2, multiply value in column 4 and column 5 by 5. Please refer appendix "Financial Planning Easy Tables" in annexure VIII for further help on working.

The amount is an indicative amount to get an idea about the investment amount needed. In the marketplace when you actually make an investment, amount of investment may vary due to minimum investment and additional investments with multiple conditions. For example, multiple investment could be in multiples of 100 and would allow you to invest amounts like 1,100, 2,400 etc. whereas multiples of 500 would not, you can invest amount like 1,000, 1,500, 2,000 etc.

Illustration 1: Amount of ₹ 1 lac needed in lump sum once at the time of admission after planning period.

Case No.	Planning Period (amount needed after – years)	Lump Sum Investment Needed Today	Regular Monthly Saving (multiply by 3 or 6 or 12 to get quarterly, half yearly or yearly saving)	Remarks
Column 1	Column 2	Column 3	Column 4	Column 5
1	10 Years	` 38560	-	Lump sum investment only
2	10 Years	19280	260	Lump sum (50%)+ regular investment(50%)
3	10 Years	-	525	Only regular investment
4	15 Years	24000	-	Lump sum investment only
5	15 Years	12000	130	Lump sum (50%)+ regular investment(50%)
6	15 Years	-	260	Only regular investment
7	20 Years	14890	-	Lump sum investment only
8	20 Years	7445	73	Lump sum (50%)+ Regular investment(50%)
9	20 Years	-	146	Only regular investment

Illustration 2: Amount of ₹ 1 lac needed for three years, from the end of planning period i.e. total 3 lac.

Case No.	Planning Period (amount needed after – years)	Lump Sum Investment Needed Today	Regular Monthly Saving (multiply by 3 or 6 or 12 to get quarterly, half yearly or yearly saving)	Remarks
Column 1	Column 2	Column 3	Column 4	Column 5
10	10 Years	105500	-	Lump sum investment only
11	10 Years	52750	715	Lump sum (50%)+ regular investment(50%)
12	10 Years		1430	Only regular investment
13	15 Years	65500	-	Lump sum investment only
14	15 Years	32750	360	Lump sum (50%)+ regular investment(50%)
15	15 Years	-	720	Only regular investment
16	20 Years	40700	-	Lump sum investment only
17	20 Years	20350	200	Lump sum (50%)+ regular investment(50%)
18	20 Years	-	400	Only regular investment

Having decided on the corpus needed one needs to draw up an investment plan. This could be a lump sum needed at the end of the planning period, or equated instalments for defined number of years, or it could be combination of both, or it could be need based.

Planning for Marriage:

Marriage is an occasion for family reunions, get-togethers and lot of rituals. It's not only a time for joy and celebrations but for expenses too. While as a parent you fulfil your responsibility of getting your kid married, the joy would be manifold if you have financially planned for it too. Though there are so many factors specific to family in planning for marriage, planning for it early will give you immense satisfaction, and like other financial goals utmost control of the situation, and your other financial goals will not be affected with the quantum of expenses.

While planning for marriage corpus you may plan for it in two parts: 1. Expenses during the marriage ceremony and 2. Expenses post marriage. Post-marriage expense planning is keeping aside an amount for post-marriage rituals, gifts, celebrations etc. It is completely up to you to decide on splitting the corpus depending upon prevalent rituals in the family.

Like other financial goals, if this goal too is planned early, it can help you in accumulating a desired sum with certainty. Let's assume that around 15 years from now you have plans for your kid's marriage, and the total one-time expenses are around 15 lac for the kind of marriage you have planned for your kid today, also you would like an additional 5 lac for post- marriage expenses.

In total at the time of marriage you would like to have a corpus of ₹ 20 lac with ₹ 15 lac for marriage and ₹ 5 lac for post marriage expenses. This amount will be invested for later use. First task therefore is to accumulate ₹ 20 lacs in today's cost. In 15 years' time the cost would go up, never forget inflation, therefore the amount needed at the end of 15 years will be much higher. Assuming inflation of 6% p.a. the amount needed to be planned at the time of marriage will be approximately ₹ 48 lac. (Please refer to "Inflation table, table 1, in appendix VIII, price of ₹ 1,000 would become ₹ 2,397 in 15 years, 20 lac therefore would become 47.94 lac ~ ₹ 48 lac) So you need to accumulate ₹ 48 lacs, out of which ₹ 36 lacs would be for marriage and ₹ 12 lacs for post marriage expenses.

With prior planning, well in advance, you would ensure that the desired sum is available - again at the cost of repeating, I have to say that delay in planning or absence of planning will not stop the rise in prices, therefore delay or absence of planning will result in lowering the expense which means compromising on your dream and lowering the quality of an event, when it could have been achieved with some prior planning.

How this sum can be made available at the time of need:

Target Corpus = ₹ 48 lac

Available time = 15 years

Choice 1 – Monthly Regular Investment
Amount to be invested every month for 15 years assuming return on investment @10% p.a.
= ₹ 12,600 (approximately)

If you start now, by investing regular sum of ₹ 12,600 per month for 15 years will get you ₹ 48 lac.

Choice 2 – One Time Investment (Lump sum)
Instead of regular investment you want to set aside lump sum amount today, then amount needed is ₹ 11.5 lac

Choice 3 – Fixed Lump Sum + Monthly Regular Investment
Or assume you have ₹ 4 lac and remaining you want to save regularly, then you need to invest ₹ 8,200 per month

Choice 4 – Fixed Monthly Regular Investment + Lump Sum Investment

Or you want to save ₹ 6,000 per month and rest in lump sum today, and then you need to invest ₹ 6 lac today

Choice 5 – Borrowing

Borrowing is also an option, but in such a situation, you may like to postpone planning for post marriage expense. If you are an employee and opted for PF then you may avail loan from your PF a/c. There is no specialised scheme of a bank or any other financial institutions to grant loan for the purpose of marriage. You can avail personal loan, loan against property or if you have gold then loan against gold. Loan amount would depend upon repayment capacity i.e. income level at the time of availing loan. The interest and principal repayment would commence almost immediately.

With the help of the simple "LIFE" principle, what looks like a mammoth task becomes easily possible. Planning makes it simple and achievable. At the cost of repetition, planning early always helps. With early planning you give more time for money to grow, you have more time to save hence with lesser amount you can save, more and above all the power of compounding works in your favour. With early planning you should get time on your side.

III. Retirement Planning

Retirement planning is one of the most ignored goals. In my experience it is considered to be a goal which is "too early to plan" and with this thinking retirement planning is kept in abeyance. One of the possible reasons for this could be the fact that retirement is perceived to be the end of working period and therefore planning for post-retirement period also gets pushed towards retirement.

You can overcome this phenomenon if you start believing that retirement is "financial freedom" and it is a time for you to pursue your own ventures, hobbies, world tours or whatever you like to do. Then you will develop an urge to create a corpus that ensures at least the same quality of life as you have today. I have observed a few of the clients have set their retirement date as early as 45 years of age.

It's my sincere advice to you to start channelling savings for retirement from the day you earn your first rupee. It is not an exaggeration of the importance of retirement planning but it is an intelligent step towards achieving financial freedom. Like other financial objectives, here too the first step is assessing the corpus needed to be accumulated for post-retirement period (This period is termed as Golden Years). This is a three step process:

Step#1 Monthly expenses estimation for Golden Years in today's cost
Step#2 Assessing monthly expenses at the time of retirement including inflation
Step#3 Calculating the lump sum amount needed at the time of retirement

You will notice that in retirement planning, the assessment in these steps is a modified replica of your current monthly expenses. Again the assessment for funds is based on funds flow pattern.

There are a few ways to assess the same, the assessment is for the amount per month needed should you retire today. It will be extrapolated to include inflation.

1. Simple Estimation Method – Assuming that your current expenses will continue post retirement too. So your present level of expenses will be the base for your savings. This method is useful for a family whose average monthly expenses is more or less stabilised. This is a very simple way to assess, however, as you know it may require a lot of fine-tuning which we'll see in other methods, but it gives you a ball park figure to begin saving and investing for your golden years.

2. Percentage Method – This method too is quite simple but quite subjective to give you an idea of expected monthly income. This method is particularly useful when your present monthly expenses are expected to rise, particularly true for those who are just starting

their career and are in an early stage of the family. Assuming your present expenses are ₹ 50,000 per month and you expect that looking at your future prospects and living standard you expect to achieve, the monthly expenses should be 50% more from this level. Therefore your base for retirement planning would be ₹ 75,000 per month.

3. Expenses Heads Method – This method requires expense heads to be defined. Broadly there are two heads of expenses in the context of retirement. First, basic expenses which, if reduced, the quality of life is also impacted considerably. Second head is discretionary expenses, which gives you the freedom to enjoy and do something that you want to do at your free will. While planning, we always try to have funds not only for basic expenses but also for discretionary expenses.

The above two methods can be applied to estimate the basic and discretionary expenses to arrive at, to calculate your post retirement average monthly expenses.

For the post retirement years-

Once the estimation for monthly expenses in today's cost is made, the second step would be to estimate what would be monthly amount at the time of retirement. The reason for such an estimate is that amount needed at the time of retirement will be substantially different owing to inflation, and since the planning period is longer the impact is more serious and very clearly visible. For example if your monthly expense estimate, based on any of the three methods in step 1, is ₹ 50,000 per month and assuming that you have planned retirement 20 years from now with 6% p.a. inflation, the amount you need in the first month of your retirement is little over ₹ 1,60,000 per month. That's whopping, but it's the hard fact too! With this rate of inflation this is the amount needed, this is the reason for planning. Again good news is that you have 20 years to accumulate to fund for your retirement.

Having estimated for expected monthly expenses, step 3 is to find targeted corpus. Since the expense at the first month of the retirement year is known, it can be assumed that the expenses will rise with the rate of inflation 6% p.a. (This is the average rate of inflation which is being assumed, a different number can be assumed based on the impact of price rise on the nature of expenses.) Another important parameter for the estimation is for how many years to be provided post-retirement. This is a technical matter and may involve complex mathematics and several assumptions, to make this discussion simple let's assume expenses to be provided for 25 years. For example if you plan to retire at the age of 60 years the expenses so planned for the age of 85th year. The planning period can vary. For example, you may plan to retire at the age of 55 years and may like to provide for 35 years of post-retirement years. The idea here is to decide retirement year and number of post retirement years to make the retirement plan complete.

Diagram showing growing monthly expenses post retirement:

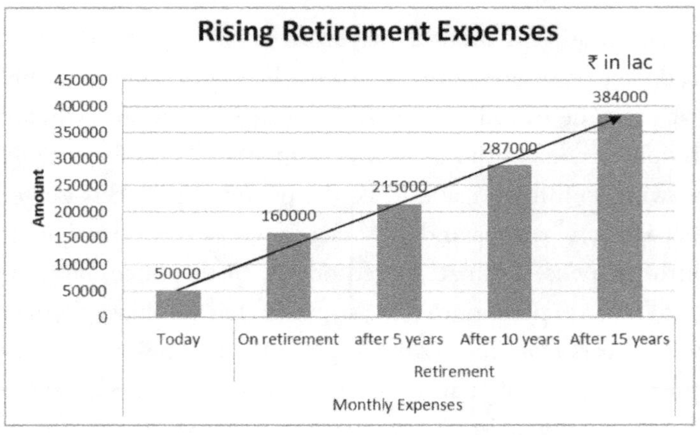

Illustration 7.4: Inflation impacts monthly expenses

Like other financial plans, in retirement planning too an investment plan can be prepared looking at funds flow requirement during the tenure. However unlike other financial goals two of its characteristics make retirement planning different than other financial goals planning. One, the planning period is much longer and application period too is longer.

There is a peculiarity in retirement planning called the retirement paradox, everyone would like to live for the longest time possible, so, financially speaking, you need funds to sustain yourself during the period. This longevity risk, the risk of "living too long" is also a risk in the parlance of retirement planning. It is just like moving in a car where fuel is sufficient to go up to 75-80 km and then, you need to go an additional 10-15 km. At 75-80 km you will run out of fuel! Just imagine, you enjoy living long but there is no money!

Continuing with the above example to provide for ₹ 1,60,000 per month for 25 years the corpus needed is near about ₹ 3.2 crore. Assuming your corpus earns returns 10% p.a. net of tax and inflation is 6% p.a., the corpus of ₹ 3.2 crore is adjusted for the inflation, i.e., in year 1, you will get ₹ 1,60,000 per month and in the second year ₹ 1,70,000 and so on.

Do not get frightened with this number, it's the fact and reality. That's why you need to plan especially to keep the living standard same as today.

And if you plan well, with appropriate asset allocation you may need to save & invest about ₹ 19.5 lac lump sum or ₹ 2,71,000 annually or ₹ 22,500 per month for this goal assuming 15% p.a. rate of return on investment. You might have noticed that unlike other financial planning goals, because of longer horizon the monthly expenses needed would also go on increasing. Continuing with the above example, a delay in planning say by 5 years will need to save & invest about ₹ 39.2 lac, (instead of ₹ 19.5 lac) lump sum or ₹ 5,83,000 (instead of ₹ 2,71,000) annually or ₹ 48,600 (instead of ₹ 22,500) per month for this goal assuming 15% p.a. rate of return on investment. Thus, procrastination is harmful, and costly too. Instead if you start planning 5 years early and you have 25 years for this goal will need to save & invest about ₹ 9.7 lac (instead of ₹ 19.5 lac) lump sum or ₹ 1,31,000 (instead of ₹ 2,71,000) annually or ₹ 10,900 (instead of ₹ 22,500) per month for this goal assuming 15% p.a. rate of return on investment. This entails the seriousness of the financial planning and substantiates the LIFE principles (**L**ong Term, **I**nvest Regularly, **F**ixed Financial Goals, **E**arly Start) start planning early. Delay or planning will not stop inflation; the cost of living would continue to go up. LIFE is the solution.

To summarise, by choice the amount of savings and investment needed towards retirement planning are:

Target Corpus = ₹ 3.2 crore
Available time = 20 years

Choice 1 – Monthly Regular Investment
Amount to be invested every month for 20 years assuming return on investment @15% p.a.
= ₹ 22,500 (approximately)

If you start now, by investing regular sum of ₹ 22,500 per month for 20 years will get you ₹ 3.2 crore.

Choice 2 – One Time Investment (Lump sum)
Instead of a regular investment you want to set aside lump sum amount today, then the amount needed is ₹ 19.5 lac

Choice 3 – Fixed Lump Sum + Monthly Regular Investment
Or assume you have ₹ 10 lac and remaining you want to save regularly then you need to invest ₹ 11,000 per month

Choice 4 – Fixed Monthly Regular Investment + Lump Sum Investment

Or you want to save ₹ 15,000 per month and rest in lump sum today, and then you need to invest ₹ 6.5 lac today

So there could be options to choose from, some other alternatives are there too drawing from other assets like reverse mortgage.

If you have other savings options going on like employer benefits, EPF or other saving schemes like PPF, then based on above choices requirement for monthly savings amount or lump sum amount would get reduced. For example if you have any of the long term savings schemes going on which at the time of retirement will give maturity amount of say ₹ 1 crore, the retirement planning amount gets reduced to ₹ 2.2 crore. With this targeted corpus you would need to save & invest about ₹ 13.5 lac lump sum or ₹ 1,87,000 annually or ₹ 15,500 per month for this goal assuming 15% p.a. rate of return on investment.

Similarly if you have pension benefits from the employer or already have some scheme which will provide regular income during the post-retirement period, than your targeted corpus will get reduced to match up the difference. However, in most of the cases the retirement benefits are not substantial enough to match up to your needs.

While planning for retirement you should asses the scope of the planning, invariably you would like to provide for your spouse too, you may like to provide for other dependents if needed. Therefore, assessing the needs and time up to which expenses need to be provided for will make your retirement planning complete.

Another important consideration is any outstanding liability which is existing or likely to come after the retirement. In such a case you need to provide for this liability too. In a nutshell your need for retirement corpus is:

Retirement Corpus = Amount towards expected expenses post retirement for self and spouse, net of existing retirement benefits (EPF/PPF, pension etc.)
+ Provision for other dependents, if needed
+ Provision for outstanding liability

What looks like a massive task becomes possible with a little planning. Your spouse and dependents will be satisfied and you will be worry free. Confidence will then speak, and you will see how LIFE works!

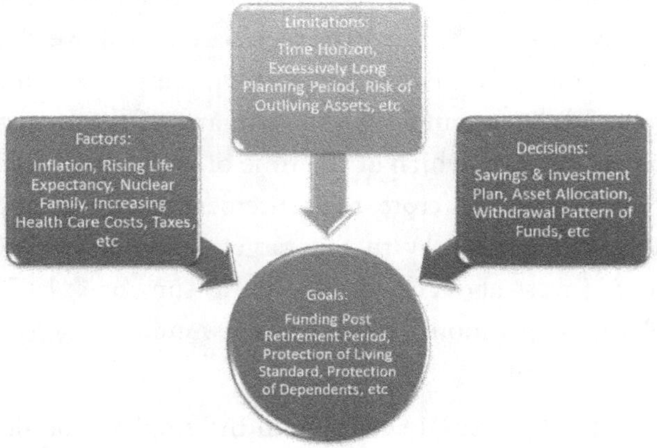

Illustration 7.5: Financial Planning for Retirement

Considerations in Retirement Planning:

1. Expenses Head – Household expenses, expenses for dependents, lifestyle expenses, health-care costs, conveyance expenses, expenses on hobbies, etc.

Assessing these expense heads and identifying their nature will help in proper estimation and help in planning. For example, healthcare expenses will go up with time because of cost escalation and with age healthcare requirements might go up. Expense for dependents may vary.

2. Post Retirement Time and Time Available for Planning – More time will help in better planning and much lesser amount would be needed for the targeted corpus. "LIFE" principles do much better in the longer horizon as also with the longer horizon you can take optimum risk with asset allocation tilted towards riskier asset classes and progressively adjusted to lower risk, thereby providing optimum returns.

3. Withdrawal Pattern & Investment Plan – The amount needed post retirement is uniformly distributed. You may need funds intermittently to discharge any outstanding liability falling due to post retirement and family responsibilities, like religious functions or rituals, or contribution to charity, or philanthropic activities. Since mostly the amount would be distributed uniformly over a very long period, an important aspect of the planning is to keep the retirement corpus invested such that it earns real positive returns.

4. Taxation – Retirement does not mean end of income tax for you, senior citizens get some tax advantages, however it does not mean that there is no tax. And also, retirement does not mean that you are in the age bracket of the senior citizens. Therefore attempt should be to manage tax to maximise post tax returns and also to assess the right amount of retirement corpus to be built, based on income available net of tax. While it is difficult to forecast tax rules and rates that will prevail during the retirement period, tax trend suggests tax rule and rates adjust somehow to inflation. Therefore, it can be safely assumed that present tax rates could be the base for planning conservatively.

Having decided on the corpus needed, you need to decide on your savings and the investment plan.

IV. Planning for Aspirational Life Goals

Having secured your family's future and planned for major life goals, it is time for planning life goals which we aspire for. As it has been said, the aim of financial planning is wealth maximisation by planning well in advance for the goals that you aspire for. Some of the goals that could be in the list of your life goals:

1. House
2. Car

3. Vacation funding
4. Farmhouse
5. Philanthropy
6. Legacy
7. Seed money for own business
8. Seed money for spouse or kids' business
9. Gifts to loved ones
10. Sponsoring religious activities
11. Wealth creation

The list can be extended to any extent and it is highly specific to an individual, therefore it depends on your aspirations. While the specific goals here may not be elaborated due to space constraints, for planning these life goals you may follow a general approach which is applicable to any of the financial goals and which have been discussed in earlier pages.

Above all, having financial goals is more important therefore you need to have some financial goal to keep yourself focused and motivated to achieve that goal. In case you do not have any tangible financial goal as of today, then decide a financial goal "wealth creation". This goal could be to accumulate say ₹ 5 lac by say 3 years. Again amount and time is important to plan resources and deciding on asset allocation. Later, the wealth creation plan can be directed to properly planned goals, even if the goals are not specifically decided, money so accumulated can be used for any of the financial goals. Money after all has so many uses.

The general steps that you may follow to plan for your life goals are:

Step # 1: Amount Needed
A prerequisite to any financial goal is to define the amount needed if the goal is to be achieved today, so that you define the goal more clearly in terms of today's cost.

Step # 2: When it is Needed
Define the timeline when the goal is best achieved. If there are multiple goals, defining them on a timeline helps in prioritising financial goals.

Step # 3: Fund Flow Pattern – Regular or one-time or a combination of regular and intermittent bullet payments and put this on the timeline by writing precise dates to the extent possible. This further helps in deciding on asset allocation and selecting the financial products.

Step # 4 Asset Allocation - Decision on asset allocation is mainly a function of time availability to save and liquidity requirements. With more time you have better flexibility on deciding on asset allocation.

Step # 5: Savings & Investment Plan – Based on above steps find how the funds would be managed from the following options A. regular savings B. one-time savings C. borrowings D. combination of A&B.

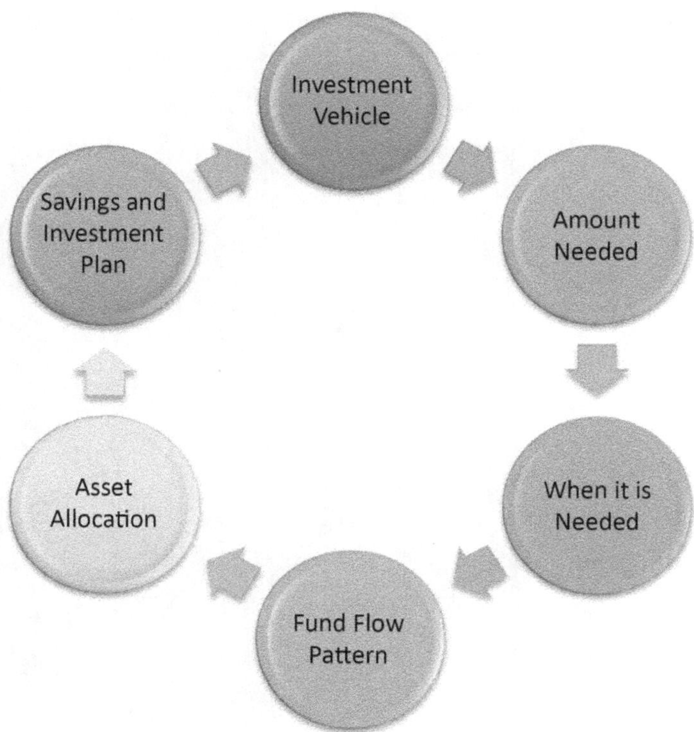

Illustration 7.6: Planning for a Financial Goal

Step # 6: Finally, towards completion of step # 5 decide on investment vehicles and if choice of options also include borrowings keep a watch for appropriate and opportune time.

Planning can get you what you have in your dream; best quality education and a dream career can be made easy with financial planning. This is mathematical, needs a little time to plan and some efforts to crystallise planning. These little steps can bring a big smile on everyone's face! Forever! This would indeed be enjoyable! Just dream and dream more!

8. Investment Avenues: Begin with Confidence

"Someone's sitting in the shade today because someone planted a tree a long time ago"
- Warren Buffett

What's an investment? An investment is deploying of savings to earn positive returns today or expected to earn positive returns in the future. An investment is always made in expectation of better returns but in the process we assume certain risks. When you do not know what could be the outcome of your investment, this is termed as risk. Deviation from expected return is risk. You may have expected a return of 12% from an investment, instead you got 14%, and this 2% deviation is a risk, however it is in your favour. If this would have been 10% instead, then this 2% would be down side risk. In our context we talk about down side risk only. Higher returns are always welcome!

When you invest you give your money to someone; this could be a bank, a financial institution, a company which is in need of funding or an intermediary who can help you in finding an investment opportunity. When you know and can manage transactions on your own you can invest directly, otherwise you need assistance either because you want to rely on the expertise of others or you do not have sufficient resources to manage on your own. We are not talking about intermediation by a broking firm or an agent but how the funds are being managed by you or by someone else.

When you buy stock through a broker you are managing funds on your own or when you are buying gold for investment purposes you are managing your own. So you have two options to invest either directly or indirectly.

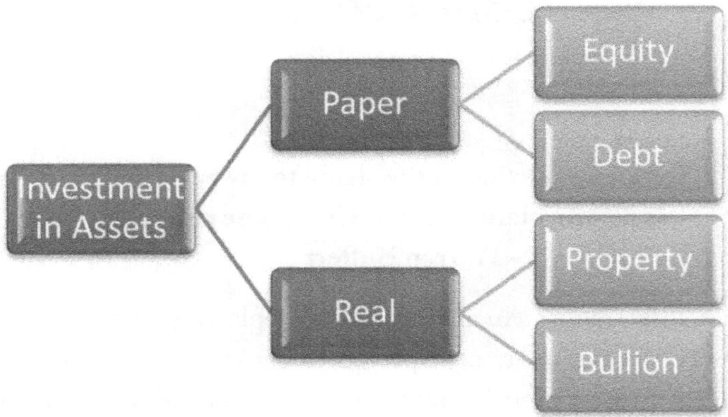

Illustration 8.1: Investment classification

Also, when you invest, what do you get against your investment? Is it something tangible or a paper? If you deposit, for example, in a bank a term deposit for 3 years for ₹ 1 lac, the bank gives you a term deposit receipt or TDR. This TDR is a paper asset. When you buy say gold for ₹ 1 lac you get physical gold (you have other forms of investing in gold too!) This gold is tangible hence called a real asset. So you have two forms of investment, paper investment and real investment.

Holding investments in paper form or real form does not make any difference as far as investment returns are concerned.

What's a portfolio?

When you decide on any investment vehicle just try to fine-tune how your money is being deployed and what type of assets are being added. When you invest over a period of time you add various assets which is called a portfolio. You might have heard on various media where experts suggest to build a diversified portfolio. They suggest to add investments which are not related. For example you should have part of your funds invested in say stocks (either directly or indirectly) part in say debt, real assets etc. this is an effective way to augment wealth and keep the risk at a certain optimum level.

In financial planning, a few terms are repetitively reminded. These are risk profile, asset allocation and goal planning. These are the foundation pillars of sound financial planning and the first step to financial planning. For achieving financial goals, an investment needs to be made and the decision on investment is the culmination of planning. With due consideration of all the facts you write a cheque in favour of a product. Surely, review and monitoring remains the key, so is revisiting financial plans, however investment decisions have direct bearing on achievement of financial plan and these decisions are longer term in nature. Therefore, investment decisions need to be taken with utmost diligence.

In my experience, being successful in investments is easier provided right decisions are taken, and these decisions are not about timing but about disciplined approach and acting upon pre-planned events or triggers rather than emotions. The major investment decision is not about investing in a particular scheme of a mutual fund or buying a govt. bond or stock of a particular company, but is asset allocation. Broadly how much investable money is being allocated is the key decision. Then follow the decisions with regard to sector within the asset class and finally a product.

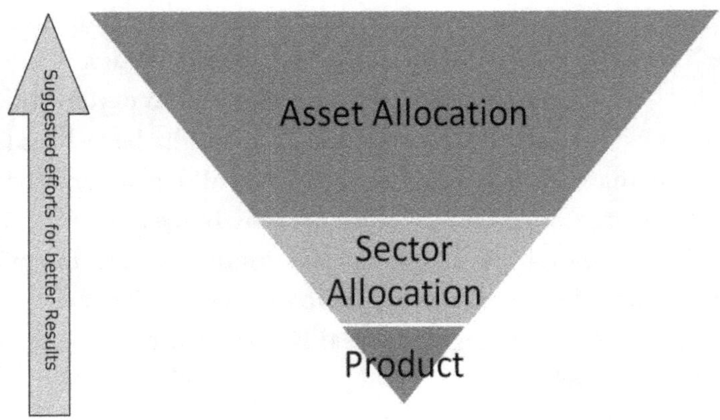

Illustration 8.2: Efforts in investment decision

While deciding more time should be given to asset allocation, followed by sector selection and finally to product selection.

What is asset allocation?

Asset allocation is deciding on % allocation of investible amount to various assets viz equity, debt, cash etc. to achieve desired financial goals.

It's a process of developing the investment portfolio. It is a bottom-up approach and can be looked upon as asset allocation for a particular goal based on tenure of the goal and summing up to assess asset allocation at holistic level based on your risk appetite within given range.

Broader Asset Classes

1. Equity – Equity as an asset class is investing in stock markets. This can be done either directly by opening an account with stock brokers or indirectly through packaged products like mutual funds, insurance ULIPs etc. Equity as an asset class has delivered highest

returns among major asset classes, considered to be highest risk bearing assets in the short run. A diversified equity portfolio for a longer period generally has given healthier positive returns. Capital appreciation is the main aim while investing in equity.

2. Debt – Also classified as Fixed Income Investment category. This category of investment has better predictability of return. Regular income mainly in the form of interest is the main aim while investing in debt. Capital appreciation too can otherwise occur due to changes in the prevalent interest rate. Major risk in such an investment will be the credit risk, i.e., probability of getting principal amount back. A diversified debt portfolio is quite less volatile than equity. Debt portfolio can be built by direct investment in tradable or non-tradable debt instruments or through schemes of mutual funds, insurance ULIPs.

3. Cash – Cash is kept in a portfolio either for foreseeable use or it has been kept in waiting for opportune time to invest. Since cash or near cash earns no returns or minimum returns, it has opportunity cost. Cash can be parked in savings bank a/c, money market mutual funds or easily redeemable short term deposits.

4. Alternative Asset – Assets which are not included above and specifically assets like real assets, commodities including precious metals, diamonds, paintings, and collectibles and hedge funds etc. are classified as alternative assets.

Let's assume Mr. X, 32 years with a family of three has three goals, Goal A, Goal B and Goal C. Goal C is wealth creation. Wealth creation is a goal which can be a goal in absence of any other defined goal, but it is better to have a goal since studies proves that anything with goal is always in sight and one strives to achieve goal unless it is completed.

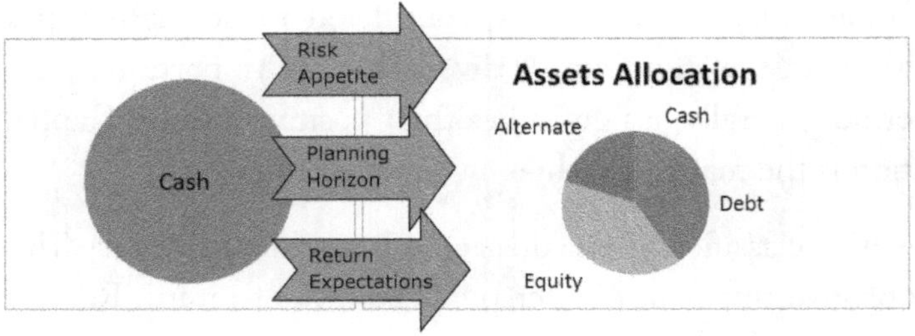

Illustration 8.3: Asset allocation

Let's assume Mr. X decides the following asset allocation, for simplicity let's assume he decides among equity, debt and cash.

Goal	Time remaining to complete, years	% of investible surplus being allocated (weight)	Equity %	Debt %	Cash %
Goal A	5	25%	0	70	30
Goal B	10	25%	60	30	10
Goal C	20	50%	100	0	0
Total	-	100%	65%	25%	10%

When we sum up the allocation it is 65% Equity, 25% Debt and 10% Cash. This can be looked at in relation to Mr. X's risk appetite and we can determine if his risk profile is in alignment with it. If it is not, we need to adjust asset allocation of the respective goals.

It is to be remembered that if goals are short term in nature, asset allocation to particular goals cannot be in risky assets hence overall asset allocation will be conservative, i.e., towards debt and cash equivalents. Therefore individual being aggressive or having appetite for risk has little meaning.

This asset allocation however is not static and it needs rebalancing, though not frequently but at a regular intervals. In the case of Mr. X after, say 4 years, asset allocation may look like this:

Goal	Time remaining to complete, years	% of investible surplus being allocated (weight)	Equity %	Debt %	Cash %
Goal A	1	25%	0	20	80
Goal B	6	25%	40	60	10
Goal C	16	50%	100	0	0
Total	-	100%	60%	20%	20%

Therefore, asset allocation would move in accordance with the goal stage. This approach has a merit over pool approach where entre investment is put in single asset allocation and amount is withdrawn as and when it is time to meet the financial needs of a goal achievement. For example, for Mr. X the appropriate allocation based on his risk profile could be,

Equity 70%, Debt 25% and Cash 5%, then investment will be made in this proportion, irrespective of goal duration, till such a time when asset allocation is changed.

Someone may find a middle path where a few goals are being allocated as per former strategy and the rest are pooled in a group. So flexibility is there and one should select a strategy which suits him better based on his own wisdom or upon advice of an expert.

Having discussed asset allocation, let's talk about these assets. The fundamental principle in investment is diversification. The major benefit of diversification is risk reduction. Without going into the mathematics of it, diversification is always suggested. If you follow the asset allocation approach based on tenure of respective financial goals, then diversification across asset classes would be achieved. You need to then diversify within the given asset class.

For example, of the total portfolio you invest say 50% of the funds to equity. Within the equity you need to diversify further. It could be in different schemes of mutual funds or equity oriented schemes of Insurance (ULIPs), or PMS or direct equity investment on your own, or combination of all these. It should be remembered that merely investing in different schemes does not ensure diversification. You need to look at the underlying portfolio before making an investment. It is possible that two schemes might be more or less investing in the same set of stock.

To recap the steps which you may follow while finally selecting a financial product:

1. Decide on asset allocation based on respective financial goals
2. Select financial products class for investment
3. Select financial product within the given class

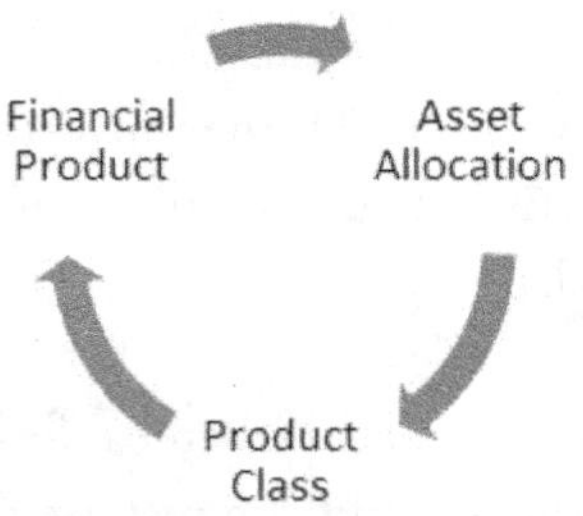

Illustration 8.4: Selecting an investment product

As discussed earlier the most important aspect in fulfilling your goal is arriving at a decision with regard to asset allocation, the remaining two steps are execution of your decision on asset allocation. Once you are sure of asset allocation, that is, what % of your investment will be made in asset classes like equity, debt, cash etc., then the next step is deciding on the product class.

Product class is a step in between asset allocation decision and finally investing your hard earned money. For example, you decide that for a particular goal you would invest say 20% amount in gold.

How would you buy gold? Let's see the possible ways to buy gold to include in your portfolio for this particular financial goal.

1. Directly buying physical gold from a jewellery showroom
2. Buying gold coins or bars from the bank
3. Buying gold units from an AMC (Mutual Fund)
4. Buy AMCs gold units of an ETF from stock exchange, in your Demat a/c
5. Buy gold fund units from an AMC (Mutual Fund) which invests in gold mining companies

You have options to choose from when it comes to investing in gold. You choose any one option or combination of these. These are product classes. Same is the case with debt or equity or any other asset classes.

Once you decide on product class then you select a financial product to finally transact. You write a cheque for a particular financial product and complete due transaction processes like KYC etc.

A few things to remember while selecting a financial product for investment, all these features are equally important and you should be having many more questions while making an investment decision, so that the decision is a well-informed investment decision; after all it is your hard earned money and no one could be a better custodian of it than you.

1. Understand the Product – A simple question to ask is whether the product under consideration is serving your purpose. Underlying risk and expected returns are in line with your estimates, and expectations and product fits in to your scheme of things, and it is working towards fulfilling your financial goal.

2. Product Features – How the funds would be utilised, form of return, whether product will be listed on stock exchanges, lock-in period, additional benefits, and flexibility to reduce or increase investment over a period of time, product taxation.

3. Product Operational Features – Basics of the product, transaction mechanism, how would you pay in, how would you withdraw money, can it be operated jointly, physical or electronic form of possession. How changes in the legal requirements or product changes will be communicated to you.

4. Legal Standing of the Product – Affiliation and or approval of the product from the appropriate regulating authority. Product disclaimers, terms and conditions, any information which is binding on you, and any condition which can withhold maturity proceeds.

5. Service Features – Service support from the product company (called as manufacturer of the product) details of branch, Brokers and Service agents' network, mode of communication like email or phone or SMS, service centre's contact details. Contact person in case query is not resolved normally.

There are a vast array of products available for an individual. Let's see some of the major financial products prevalent in India.

(How to use this section: A product category can serve different asset classes. For example mutual funds can serve as equity or debt or near cash depending on the scheme of the fund, therefore mutual fund as an investment category needs to be matched with the targeted asset allocation. For each of the product category possible asset class has been indicated which could be equity, debt, cash and alternate asset. Also summaries with the table and chart for easy comprehension and effective decision making)

With time the product choice is broadening, with more products to choose from and with better customisation today, a 'better fit' could be obtained. However this also leads to some chaos while trying to select a product from the variety of products available today. With the advent of technology trading facilities, transaction details, portfolio details etc. are available on your smart phone at your will. With increasing touch points, sometimes companies which are aggressive in leveraging marketing may pose as ideal fit, which may not be the case. Therefore, product selection is a job that needs your full attention and a detailed analysis based on parameters specific to you like your financial goals, financial priorities and liabilities, age, family income, number of dependents etc.

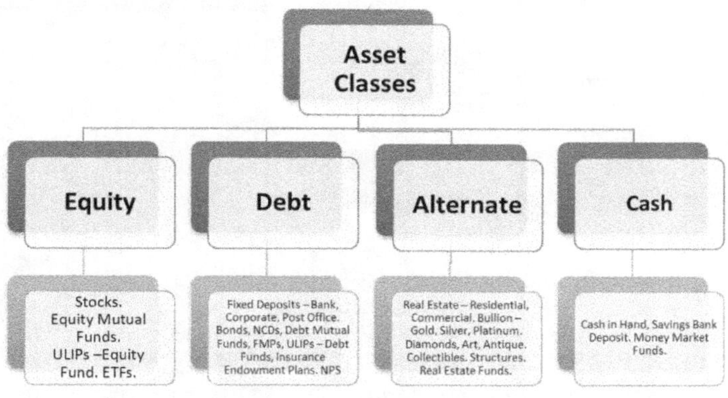

Illustration 8.5: Asset Classes

1. Equity Stocks (Asset Category: Equity) – An equity stock or equity share is a share in the capital of a company. When you buy a stock of a company you become business owner to the extent of stocks you own. As an investor your aim is not to really own a company but get the benefits of owning a successful company or an 'expected to be' successful company. Therefore you should select from a wider variety of listed stocks on stock exchanges.

If you are confident of selecting right stocks this is an investment which rewards investors handsomely. This is a direct investment and you can buy and sell stocks through a trading account with a stock broker either in primary market (like IPO) or secondary market (listed stocks).

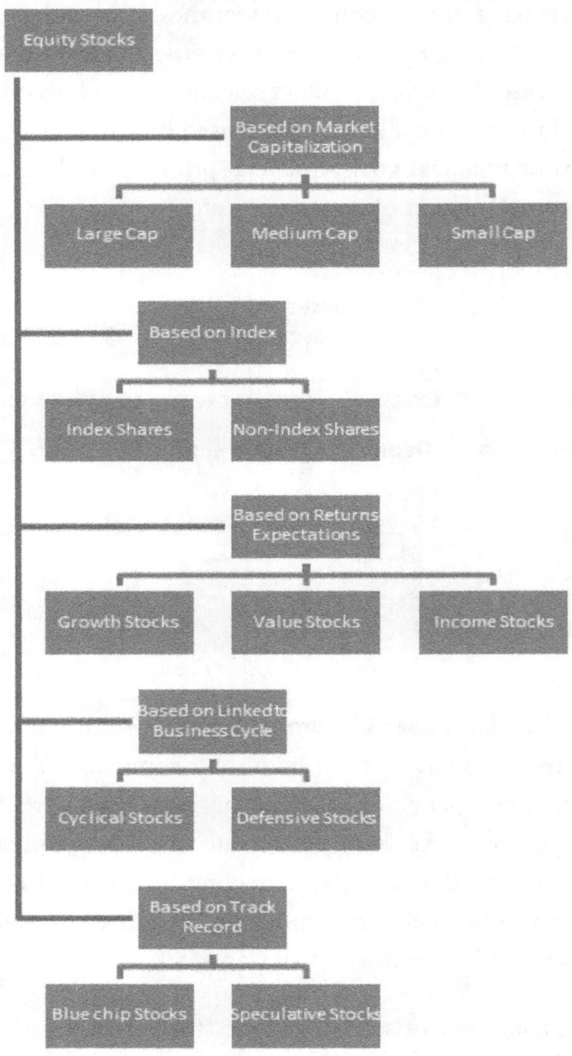

Illustration 8.6 Equity Classification: Equity classification is indicative and there could be many more criteria to classify equity stocks.

For a longer horizon, equity investment is recommended and here too diversification is the key. You should build a diversified portfolio with 4-5 sectors and 2-3 companies in each of the chosen sectors.

There is loads of information available about dos and don'ts of equity stock investment; a few of them are:

i. Always keep a diversified portfolio of stocks
ii. Know the risk
iii. Buy stock with good fundamentals, do not buy or sell on tips, rumors etc.
iv. Do not trade if you are investing and do not invest if you are trading
v. Expect reasonable returns, do not speculate

2. Equity Derivatives (Asset Category: Equity) – The common derivatives available in equity markets are equity futures and equity options. These are leveraged instruments which gives larger exposure for a defined period of time. These are instruments meant for risk management. The price at which transaction takes place depends on the underlying security, nature of the derivative and other market factors. For example value of index future would depend on current value of the index, contract month and market sentiments.

In addition to risk hedging, it could offer you arbitrage opportunities too which are mostly encashed by institutions and bigger traders. However there are speculators in the market who participate in the trading of derivatives in a big way. One can earn returns if they understand the inherent risk appropriately. The equity derivatives are traded on stock exchanges.

From the financial planning point of view it is advisable that equity derivatives are used as a risk management tool with a great amount of caution and proper understanding.

3. Commodity Derivatives (Asset Category: Alternate) – Like equity derivatives the value of commodity derivatives is derived from the underlying commodity. Commodity trading has gained momentum in India from the last decade. There are various categories of commodities like precious metals, metals, agricultural commodity, energy and other commodities. Understanding commodity valuation is comparatively easier, at the same time commodity markets are very dynamic too. These are also leveraged products and for longer term position you need to keep rolling the contract.

4. Mutual Funds (Asset Category: Equity, Debt, Cash & Alternative) – Mutual funds offer an opportunity to participate in virtually any asset class with a little sum of money. It can be understood as investment schemes managed on your behalf for a fee by investment professionals. When you decide to invest through a mutual fund you look at the schemes under which you want to invest, that scheme has well defined scheme objectives and indicated portfolio of investment. Eventually you invest in a scheme of mutual fund considering its performance, AMC, fund manager etc. Mutual funds offer a variety of schemes, and they offers various benefits like:

A. Professionally-managed funds
B. Wider choice of schemes
C. Very well regulated industry
D. Diversification benefits
E. Good liquidity
F. Reasonably lower cost

There are numerous schemes offered by the mutual funds. Basically these schemes are classified based on where the funds are invested and whether & how the income is distributed.

In addition to regular schemes, mutual funds also offer Exchange Traded Funds or ETFs. These funds mimic the underlying and are traded on the stock exchanges like stocks. For example index ETF will reflect the underlying index. For a long term investment these ETFs are quite handy. You get to invest in the entire portfolio with even a small amount of money

Another way which makes investment in mutual funds more attractive is systematic investment plan or SIP. Based on your need you have an option to invest in selected scheme at a regular interval say monthly. This is a powerful tool which helps in wealth creation but you need to have a long term view and keep saving through SIPs over a longer horizon.

5. Bank Fixed Deposit (Asset category: Debt) – Bank fixed deposit or FD, also called as term deposits have been quite popular for ages. It has been considered to be the one of the most reliable investments with certainty and peace of mind. At the same time, from the perspective of understanding, these products are quite easy to comprehend. You need to choose the tenure for which you want to make a deposit, and you get the interest rate applicable and during the tenure of the deposit your income, i.e., interest rate is locked, and you get that for sure. Typically deposit tenure is available from a fortnight to 5 years. It is up to you to opt for regular interest payout or cumulative deposit. Interest on such deposits of a bank is generally quarterly compounding.

Another product which is available for regular savings is the Recurring Deposit or RD where you decide to deposit a regular amount every month for a fixed tenure normally 2 to 3 years. This is also a good way to build a smaller corpus for a shorter term.

The bank products for investment are quite popular because of:

1. Very Simple Product – It is easy to understand fixed income banking products, the simplicity feature makes it a choice for many investors
2. Accessibility – Easy to approach a bank, this makes transaction easy with peace of mind
3. Familiarity – Regular interactions with the bank for routine financial transactions, this makes an individual familiar with banking environment and products
4. Easy Transaction – It is a matter of habit, because you already have some transaction with a bank, so it becomes another routine bank transaction

5. Liquidity – Investment can be liquidated at very short notice and in most of the cases instantaneously
6. Technology – Net banking, mobile banking, ATMs, call centres have made banking transactions further convenient

There are more products available with the bank with above two as the base products. For those having salary account or business account with a bank they get some other transaction facilities too, to make investment further attractive or convenient.

Nowadays banks also sell mutual funds and insurance; these are called third party products. Here the bank is acting as an intermediary or an agent. These are not bank products.

6. Corporate Fixed Deposits (Asset category: Debt) – Corporate or Company Fixed Deposits are also very prevalent among investors. As the name suggests, these deposits are made in companies like manufacturing companies, non-banking financial companies or NBFCs, Housing finance companies. These are fixed income investments where you get fixed percentage of interest income on principal amount and principal amount is either returned back or renewed further. These are not listed or traded like bonds.

On these deposits interest rate is higher than bank deposits. Compound of interest also varies from scheme to scheme, it could be monthly, quarterly, half yearly or yearly. While investing do pay attention to compounding as it may impact effective yield.

These deposits are riskier than bank deposits as return of interest and principal amount depends on the financial health of a company. Before investing in company deposits you must see the credit rating of the company and keep watch on the credit rating of the company. Company deposit may not offer the same flexibility as a bank and for premature withdrawal you may need to wait for some days, particularly for manufacturing companies.

These deposits are mostly facilitated by investment advisory firms or individual investment advisors. Please remember all the company deposits are not at par, some companies are very strong in their financials while some may not be so. Therefore while investing in company deposits, be vigilant to get the benefit of higher interest rates.

Diagram: Company Deposits

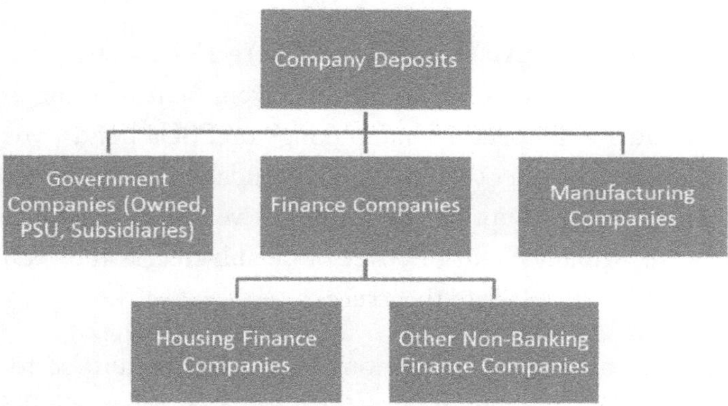

Broad Spectrum of Company Deposits: Look for rate of interest, frequency of compounding, tenure, lock-in period, credit rating, ease of operation, track record and add-on features.

7. Tradable Bonds & NCDs (Asset category: Debt) – These are also fixed income investments with an additional feature of tradability. These are issued mostly by private companies. As the name suggests these are instruments which are listed and traded on stock exchanges. Therefore with the benefits of fixed income investment and this additional benefit, you can sell the bonds on the exchange or buy when you need to invest, hence entry and exit is much better. Only thing you need to look at is whether the exchange bond has the liquidity to allow you to buy or sell.

Interest on these bonds and NCD vary with credit rating, tenure and bond features like cumulative interest or regular interest payment etc. and interest on these bonds is higher than bank fixed deposits. In some cases when you subscribe to these bonds you may also get listing gains.

Compared to non-tradable fixed income investment, tradable bonds offer superior interest rate risk management. The bond value will go up with the lower market interest rate and vice-versa.

8. GOI & PSUs Bonds (Asset category: Debt) – Debt investments have quite a wide variety of options with Government of India or GOI bonds and Public Sector Undertakings or PSUs bonds: you have more options to choose from. GOI bonds and PSU bonds are also good investment options for conservative investment since these bonds are virtually credit risk-free or default free, as the GOI or GOI backed institutions are the issuers.

The government-sponsored institutions like infrastructure sector companies, housing development companies and other similar institutions in priority sector issue bonds at regular intervals. Quite often these bonds offer tax benefits also like tax free bonds. With these features sometimes it becomes attractive investment options in debt category. These bonds may also be listed which provides further benefit of liquidity too.

State government and state government sponsored institutions also regularly issue bonds at attractive interest rates. Investment advisory companies facilitate subscription to these instruments.

9. Post Office Savings Schemes (Asset category: Debt) – Post offices offer a range of debt investment options. National Savings Certificates or NSCs are quite popular and have been so for a long time. These are mostly small savings offered primarily to augment small savings and for better financial inclusion, therefore it may have upper cap on maximum investment amount. The post office schemes may offer tax benefits also but all schemes of post office savings do not offer tax benefits.

Some of The popular Post Office savings schemes are

A. NSC – There are two types of NSCs at present, these are 5 Years National Savings Certificate (VIII Issue) and 10 Years National Savings Certificate (IX Issue). NSCs are issued at face value and redeemed at the end of the tenure with cumulative amount of interest and principal. Interest on NSCs are monthly compounded and available in the denominations of ₹ 100, ₹ 500, ₹ 1,000, ₹ 5,000 and ₹ 1,000.

B. Monthly Income Scheme (MIS) – This is 5-year scheme with the interest payable monthly. In this scheme you pay a lump sum amount at the beginning and you get monthly interest and you get principal amount back at the maturity. That maximum amount for single account holder is ₹ 4.5 lac and joint account holder is ₹ 9 lac.

C. 5 Year Recurring Deposit – This is 5 year account extendable to 5 year period on maturity. There no maximum limit on amount that can be deposited monthly with minimum amount being ₹ 10 and in the multiple of ₹ 5s.

D. Post office Fixed Deposit – These are post office time deposits available for 1 year, 2 years, 3 years and 5 years tenure. Again to facilitate small savings the minimum amount with which a time deposit account can be opened is ₹ 200.

E. Senior Citizen Savings Scheme - This is a specific scheme for senior citizens of the age 60 years and above. The scheme has maturity period of 5 years which can be extended to further 3 years with 1 year of maturity. The interest rate on this deposit is higher than other post office schemes by around 1% with income tax benefits. The maximum amount which can be deposited under this scheme is capped at ₹ 15 lac.

In addition the post office also offers savings account, 15 Year PPF account and insurance.

10. Life Insurance Schemes (Asset Category: Equity/Debt) – Insurance, as said by the experts is the most popular product which is least understood. These instruments could be a very powerful tool in protection, wealth building, tax planning and estate planning. Life insurance product comes with lock in period and these are products for long term.

For the same insurance cover premium may differ from insurance company to company. You need to compare the product and price before buying it. A very generic classification of life insurance products categorises them into four classes:

1. Pure Protection – In this category the premium paid towards life insurance policy goes for protection only and no component of premium goes towards savings. Therefore on maturity of the policy, the policyholder does not get any maturity amount. Term plans, for example are pure protection plans.

In pure protection, the premium paid can be termed as the cost of insurance. The premium paid towards life insurance goes up with increasing age.

2. Endowment – In this category along with pure protection, savings are added. It can be said to be a package of insurance and savings. A part of the premium goes towards the protection and other part goes towards investment in debt. The investment earns returns as bonus declared by the company annually. The policy holder gets this

amount back either on maturity or intermittently as per the policy terms.

Variation in life cover like extended life cover, return of invested amount at maturity or in the last 4 years or every 4 years etc. provide varieties in endowment products. Endowment plans come with different names and these products are quite popular and prevalent. From the asset allocation perspective it is debt investment.

3. ULIP – The Unit Linked Insurance Plans or ULIPs are plans which invest savings in predetermined schemes of funds. In this type of policies a part of the premium goes towards protection and other part is invested based on preference of the policy holder. The investment could be made in equity schemes, debt schemes, cash schemes or a combination of these. On selecting any of the options of investment, units are allotted to the policy holders at the prevailing rate.

ULIP plans are quite flexible and transparent in funds management. The returns are quite visible to policy holders at any time and one can see the same by looking at net value of units allotted. Policy holder also has option to change the investment option.

4. Other Plans – there are other plans which are offered by life insurance companies like retirement plans, health plans, and group plans etc.

11. Special Savings Scheme (Category: Debt/Equity) – There are other schemes too which may suit your requirement and fit into your overall financial goal planning - to mention two of the schemes:

A. 15 Year Public Provident Fund – This scheme also popularly known as PPF, has 15 years tenure extendable to further 5 years and is for long terms savings. The account can be opened at designated banks or post offices. In a financial year maximum amount that can be deposited in PPF is limited to ₹ 1.5 lacs with minimum amount to be deposited being ₹ 500.

PPF offers tax benefits on investment and interest earned, this is in addition to the fact that it is virtually credit risk free being a government backed scheme. Partial withdrawal and loan facility makes it a little flexible too.

B. National Pension System – NPS is an initiative of the PFRDA which aims at promoting old age income security. NPS is a defined contribution plan for retirement and voluntarily extended to citizens of India between 18 years to 60 years of age. When you open an account under the NPS you get tier I account which is a non-withdrawal account with tax benefits. You need to open the account with a minimum of ₹ 500 and in a year the minimum contribution is ₹ 6,000. You have an option to open tier-II account, which is optional savings and you can withdraw the amount from this account at your will. You can open a tier-II account with ₹ 1,000.

NPS is probably the lowest cost system in its class with flexibility. In NPS you have an option to select a fund manager who will manage the funds from the following two investment options:

A. Active Choice - Choice of funds from Asset Class E which is predominantly equity market oriented, asset class C which is predominantly non-government fixed income investments and the asset class G which is investment in government securities. In asset class E you can invest up to a maximum of 50% whereas you can choose to invest up to 100% in asset class C or asset class G.

B. Auto Choice – In this choice the investment will be made in the Life Cycle fund which will invest funds in asset classes C, G and E in predetermined proportions according to your age and keep on changing with increasing age.

You can change your investment option and asset allocation ratio once in a financial year. These investments are subject to market risk. You can withdraw the accumulated wealth on attaining the age of 60 years; you have to utilise at least 40% of the accumulated wealth in annuity purchase from a recognised annuity service provider. The annuity service provides you with regular income for a defined period of time as opted by you. You have an option to withdraw the accumulated wealth before attaining the age of 60 years also.

12. Real Estate (Category: Alternate) – Real estate investment is also a very popular mode of investment in India. It needs quite a large chunk of investment at one go and one needs to appraise the property with utmost diligence. Real estate deals and negotiations are an art in itself.

You can buy residential property, plots, and commercial property to get rental income or sell it later for profit. Investors adopt different strategies to invest in real estate based on their experience and availability of funds

1. Buying under construction properties and selling it on completion at market premium
2. Buying commercial and residential property for rental yield
3. Buying residential or commercial property for capital appreciation in the longer term
4. Buying residential plots developed by development authorities

Since there is a regulated real estate market and every piece of property is unique the price discovery is an onerous task. You may need to scan through a good number of properties before a few are shortlisted for final negotiations.

13. Bullion (Category: Alternate) – Nothing much needs to be written about investment in bullion, particularly gold, for Indians. Savings are invariably spent on buying gold. It has been a tradition in India and we all trust in gold during volatile periods. This is what makes India the largest consumer of gold. This is a product which is probably comprehended by almost all members of a family.

Bullion is also part of commodities; in addition to investment in gold you have an option to invest in silver and platinum also. You can buy bullion in physical form like coins, bars or also in electronic form like ETF and units of mutual funds. From an investment perspective, bullion fetches positive returns in the longer run but it does exhibit volatility too.

14. Structured Products (Category: Alternate) – Structured products are market linked which could be combinations of equity, derivatives, debt and cash equivalents. These are a packaged strategies with a structured outcome.

One of the commonly preferred structures is capital guarantee investment. The structure offers protection of principal on maturity and gives an opportunity to participate in the positive returns of the underlying. There are several types of structures available in the market through wealth management firms and normally the ticket size of these investments is higher.

Structures help in meeting specific investment needs like protection of capital, return participation in underlying security in a defined proportion etc. and these are an alternative investment. These investments can help in managing risk and could help in building a healthier portfolio.

15. Investing in Art, Antiques & Collectibles (Category: Alternate) – Investing in art, antiques and collectibles needs good amount of exposure, patience and passion too. With this prerequisite these could be a profitable investment option in addition to building a diversified investment portfolio.

Good quality art does appreciate with time, however it is susceptible to wide fluctuations so inherent risk is comparatively higher. Looking at the size of the investment needed, it is prudent for an investor with higher investible surplus to explore investing in this category of investment. Art funds, which is turn invests in art could be another option.

16. Investing in Business (Category: Alternate) – An investment avenue prudent to be explored by those investors with higher net worth is investing in businesses. Investment bankers and investment intermediaries help in identifying investment opportunities in growing business sectors. Private equity, venture funding, buying business stakes and angel investing are a few options to explore for higher risk investment opportunity with potentially higher returns.

These investments are available as packages from venture funds or also individually which is evaluated on case to case basis, with the assistance of an expert investment advisory firm.

The choice of a product for achieving your financial goal depends on the suitability of a product which is very specific to an individual. The key is to find a product that is a right fit as well as very specific to your financial goals. It is always advisable to look for good opportunity to invest but you should never change or build a financial goal based on an investment product. Financial products are here to help you realise your goal. You should make use of it profitably to achieve your life goals!

9. Financial Planning Diary: Written Commitment

"Reduce your plan to writing. The moment you complete this, you will have definitely given concrete form to the intangible desire"
- Napoleon Hill

There is a famous saying "Write it on Stamp Paper", i.e., give a firm commitment. In financial planning too writing goals and monitoring progress to achieve those goals is more important and have direct impact on final achievement of financial goals.

Here is your personal financial planning diary. Make a commitment to yourself to achieve your financial goals, record transactions and monitor on your own how much you are closer to your financial goals.

Why this diary?

Many a time when we are in need of a special document, (special because it is needed and it is always last moment) it is hard to find. Except for that important piece of paper or information we find everything else. There are certain important papers or information which have to be kept in a safer place and in such a way that in case of need they can be retrieved and used exactly as needed.

The record-keeping must be given due weightage which could be physical storage or electronic storage with a backup. There are certain records which need to be noted & checked appropriately and regularly, like transactions which are to be included in income tax returns, standing instructions, ECS, redemption of an investment etc. In addition there are certain transactions which need to be checked, though not very routine but important like change of address, change of nomination, change in mandate, change in bank account etc.

Record of financial transactions, like bank statements, contract notes, premium receipts, investment statements etc. are not only important to know current valuation and tax assessment but also for resolving any dispute or arbitration, in case it comes across as an evidence.

Though focus here is on keeping the record of financial transactions, equally important is furnishing correct information and checking it thoroughly. Correctness of postal address, bank account number, email ID, telephone number, mobile number, nomination etc. also wherever this information is shared that also needs to be recorded. Any changes in these particulars need to be updated at every place.

For better management of selected financial goals it is a must to keep track of all relevant financial transactions to facilitate optimum management of financial goals viz. for an investment, directed to a particular goal, changes in the underlying investment like if it is debt investment then date of interest payment, current valuation, if tradable etc. would be needed for portfolio valuation and review. For investment in mutual fund, say through SIP, record of SIP date, standing instructions, dividend declared etc. should be updated and tallied. Insurance, life or non-life, for example, date of premium payment should be adhered to.

These are a few examples which suggest that the transaction alone is not sufficient; its record and maintaining due date of upcoming transactions is also equally important. Your advisors should also facilitate you; however you need to rely on yourself for better control of your financial goals.

Part – I Physical Record Creation

Records of transactions and documentary evidences are needed for several purposes though these are not just limited to facilitate financial transactions. Proper record keeping is an essential supplement to financial planning. It not only helps in fulfilling the purpose for which financial planning has been done but gives great peace of mind.

Though requirement of record keeping varies from individual to individual, this diary will assist you in keeping record of your financial transactions to some extent. You can record financial transactions and important information in this diary and keep physical record separately, by making files. To organise these files you may create one master index, as suggested below:

File No.	File Title	Contents	Record Tenure	Review Frequency	Important Date
1	Identity Documents	Passport copy, PAN copy, Election Card, Aadhar Card, credit card, driving license	Always	Once a year for renewal update, if any	
2	Address Records	Electricity bills, bank statements etc., in addition to identity documents	Last 1 year	Once in a quarter	
3.	Academic Records	Mark sheets, certificates, diploma, degree certificates	Always	Once a year to organise records	
4.	Banking Transactions	Bank passbook, bank statement (can be maintained electronically), cheque books	1 year	Once a month	
5.	Insurance Record	Life insurance policies, medical policies, vehicle insurance, other insurance policies, advisor's contact number, insurance company's helpline / contact numbers	Always, till the policies are in force	Once in a quarter, mark renewal/due date	
6.	Investment Record	Fixed deposit receipts, mutual fund statements, equity shares holding, other investments, advisory, brokers' contact numbers, DP book, KYC records	Always	Once in a quarter	

File No.	File Title	Contents	Record Tenure	Review Frequency	Important Date
7.	Bills & Payables	Credit card, Loan record, overdraft, property tax, etc.	Till the time in force	Once in a month	
8.	Tax Records	Tax returns and supporting	Always	Once in six months	
9.	Home & Real Estate	Registration documents, contracts, POA	Always	Once in six months	
10.	Estate & Other Records	Copy of will, charity, lending, cancelled cheques, contracts, trust details	Need based	Once in six months	

The record keeping should add to one's convenience and one can create records in his own way. The idea here is to organise important financial transactions so that in case of need the desired information is easily retrievable.

Also, one can add a reminder for important events in the index file to make it more useful.

Formats covered in this chpater can be downloaded from the website www.authorvinaymahajan.com

Part II - A Let's write your Financial Goals as a sign of commitment towards achieving them

Financial Goal No.1

- Priority ranking:
- Financial goal:
- Date by when to be achieved:
- Present cost, Rs:
- Amount needed at the time of goal fulfillment, Rs:
- Amount available as of today, Rs:
- Amount needed further, Rs:
- Remarks:

Financial Goal No.2

- Priority ranking:
- Financial goal:
- Date by when to be achieved:
- Present cost, Rs:
- Amount needed at the time of goal fulfillment, Rs:
- Amount available as of today, Rs:
- Amount needed further, Rs:
- Remarks:

Financial Goal No.3

- Priority ranking:
- Financial goal:
- Date by when to be achieved:
- Present cost, Rs:
- Amount needed at the time of goal fulfillment, Rs:
- Amount available as of today, Rs:
- Amount needed further, Rs:
- Remarks:

Financial Goal No.4

- Priority ranking:
- Financial goal:
- Date by when to be achieved:
- Present cost, Rs:
- Amount needed at the time of goal fulfillment, Rs:
- Amount available as of today, Rs:
- Amount needed further, Rs:
- Remarks:

Financial Goal No.5

- Priority ranking:
- Financial goal:
- Date by when to be achieved:
- Present cost, Rs:
- Amount needed at the time of goal fulfillment, Rs:
- Amount available as of today, Rs:
- Amount needed further, Rs:
- Remarks:

Financial Goal No.6

- Priority ranking:
- Financial goal:
- Date by when to be achieved:
- Present cost, Rs:
- Amount needed at the time of goal fulfillment, Rs:
- Amount available as of today, Rs:
- Amount needed further, Rs:
- Remarks:

Financial Goal No.7

- Priority ranking:
- Financial goal:
- Date by when to be achieved:
- Present cost, Rs:
- Amount needed at the time of goal fulfillment, Rs:
- Amount available as of today, Rs:
- Amount needed further, Rs:
- Remarks:

Financial Goal No.8

- Priority ranking:
- Financial goal:
- Date by when to be achieved:
- Present cost, Rs:
- Amount needed at the time of goal fulfillment, Rs:
- Amount available as of today, Rs:
- Amount needed further, Rs:
- Remarks:

Financial Goal No.9

- Priority ranking:
- Financial goal:
- Date by when to be achieved:
- Present cost, Rs:
- Amount needed at the time of goal fulfillment, Rs:
- Amount available as of today, Rs:
- Amount needed further, Rs:
- Remarks:

Financial Goal No.10

- Priority ranking:
- Financial goal:
- Date by when to be achieved:
- Present cost, Rs:
- Amount needed at the time of goal fulfillment, Rs:
- Amount available as of today, Rs:
- Amount needed further, Rs:
- Remarks:

Part II-B Financial Goal Status as of 1st April

Once you initiate investment for a particular financial goal, it is imperative to track achievement of goals, just like in a cricket match, when a team chases for runs to win the game. The target run rate is known at the beginning, after a few bowling overs based on scored runs, the asking run rate may change. Updating goal status is a must to reassess and decide on next course of strategy. This gives a snap shot and there is no need to review it too frequently unless the goal date is near.

A. Goal Stage

Financial Goal Number	Financial Goal	Priority Rank	Current Status (Goal Stage) P, I, C, A, N	Date When First Thought About It
1				
2				
3				
4				
5				
6				
7				
8				
9				
10				

P - Planned, I - Initiated, C - Corpus Accumulated,
A - Achieved, N - Not Planned

B. Goal Status

Financial Goal Number	Financial Goal	Start Date	Target Date	Corpus Needed on Target Date (Approximate valuation)	Amount Available
1					
2					
3					
4					
5					
6					
7					
8					
9					
10					

Part III. Existing Investment Details – As on 1st April

A. Equity Shares

Broker's Name (1)______________________________

Demat Account Number________________________

Relationship Manager__________________________

Contact Number______________________________

Broker's Name (2)______________________________

Demat Account Number________________________

Relationship Manager__________________________

Contact Number _____________________________

Summary of Segment

(Amount, Rs lac)

Segment	Broker 1	Broker 2
Equity		
Equity F&O		
Commodity		
MFSS		
Cash		
TOTAL		

Record of equity shares will help to track performance of your investment, and knowing about your equity investment better, in addition to knowing tax implications from the short term gain or long term gain point of view. Record equity shares which are held as investments. You may like to keep trading records separately.

Scrip Name	Number of Shares	Buying Date	Buying Price, Rs	Current Price, Rs (Use Pencil)

B. Mutual Funds – (i) Lump Sum Investment

Advisor's Name (1)______________________________

Contact Number_________________________________

Advisor's Name (2)______________________________

Contact Number_________________________________

Folio Number/s ________________________

Scheme Name	Number of Units	Date of Transactions	Buying NAV, Rs	Current / Transaction NAV, Rs

(ii) Systematic Investment Plan (SIP) as on 1st April

Folio Number/s ______________________________

Scheme Name / Scrip Name	SIP Date	SIP Amount, Rs	No of Units/ Shares	Current Valuation, Rs

C. Life Insurance as on 1st April

Advisor's Name (1)______________________________

Contact Number______________________________

Advisor's Name (2)______________________________

Contact Number______________________________

Policy Details	Date of Transaction	Insurance Cover Amount, Rs	Premium amount, Rs	Date of Payment	Maturity Date	Maturity Amount, Rs

D. Non - Life or General Insurance Details as on 1st April

Advisor's Name (1)______________________________

Contact Number______________________________

Advisor's Name (2)______________________________

Contact Number______________________________

Policy Name	Date of Transaction	Insurance Cover Amount, Rs	Premium amount, Rs	Renewal Payment Date	Coverage Date Up To

E. Fixed & Recurring Deposits as on 1st April

Advisor's Name (1)________________________________

Contact Number__________________________________

Advisor's Name (2)________________________________

Contact Number__________________________________

Deposit Details	Date of Transaction	Amount, Rs	Tenture, Years	Interest, %	Maturity Amount, Rs	Maturity Date	Bank A/C Affiliated

F. Gold Investment as on 1st April

Mode of Investment (Lump sum, SIPs, Occasionally)	Date of Investment	Type of Fund (ETF, Gold Fund of AMC, Fund of Fund, Physical gold)	Total Units / Quantity, gm	Current Valuation, Rs

Part IV Outstanding Loans and Borrowings

EMI Date	Loan Details	Loan Amount, Rs	EMI amount, Rs	Bank / NBFC / Agency

Part V Financial Transactions (During the Year 1 Apr to 31 Mar)

Date	Transaction Details	Amount, Rs	Transaction (Buy/ Sell/Other)	Broker/Agency

Date	Transaction Details	Amount, Rs	Transaction (Buy/ Sell/Other)	Broker/Agency

Date	Transaction Details	Amount, Rs	Transaction (Buy/Sell/Other)	Broker/Agency

Date	Transaction Details	Amount, Rs	Transaction (Buy/ Sell/Other)	Broker/Agency

Date	Transaction Details	Amount, Rs	Transaction (Buy/ Sell/Other)	Broker/Agency

Date	Transaction Details	Amount, Rs	Transaction (Buy/ Sell/Other)	Broker/Agency

Date	Transaction Details	Amount, Rs	Transaction (Buy/ Sell/Other)	Broker/Agency

Part – VI Important Contacts to remember

Contact Group	Contact Person	Contact Number	Mail ID
Broker/Advisor			
CAs/Lawyer/Real Estate Consultant			

Contact Group	Contact Person	Contact Number	Mail ID
Banking			
Miscellaneous Consultants/ Advisor (Forex, MoneyTransfer, Gold, Alternative Investments)			
Other Contacts			

Part – VII Important Document Numbers to Remember

(You may use reference number to maintain secrecy)

Particular	Number	Agency / Company	Renewal Date, if applicable
PAN Card			
Savings A/c 1			
Savings A/c 2			
Savings A/c 3			
Bank Locker 1			
Bank Locker 2			
DEMAT A/c 1			
DEMAT A/c 2			
DEMAT A/c 3			

Particular	Number	Agency / Company	Renewal date, if applicable
PMS DMAT a/c			
Credit Card 1			
Credit Card 2			
Debit Card			
Debit Card			
Aadhar card			
Aadhar Card			

Part – VIII Important Events/Dates to Remember

Month - January

S. No.	Event	Date/Due Date	Priority

Important Events/Dates to Remember

Month - February

S. No.	Event	Date/Due Date	Priority

Important Events/Dates to Remember

Month - March

S. No.	Event	Date/Due Date	Priority

Important Events/Dates to Remember

Month - April

S. No.	Event	Date/Due Date	Priority

Important Events/Dates to Remember

Month - May

S. No.	Event	Date/Due Date	Priority

Important Events/Dates to Remember

Month - June

S. No.	Event	Date/Due Date	Priority

Important Events/Dates to Remember

Month - July

S. No.	Event	Date/Due Date	Priority

Important Events/Dates to Remember

Month - August

S. No.	Event	Date/Due Date	Priority

Important Events/Dates to Remember

Month - September

S. No.	Event	Date/Due Date	Priority

Important Events/Dates to Remember

Month - October

S. No.	Event	Date/Due Date	Priority

Important Events/Dates to Remember

Month - November

S. No.	Event	Date/Due Date	Priority

Important Events/Dates to Remember

Month - December

S. No.	Event	Date/Due Date	Priority

Appendices

Appendix – I

Some of the websites for information on financial services

- www.moneycontrol.com
- www.amfiindia.com
- www.camsonline.com
- www.karvymfs.com
- www.valueresearchonline.com
- www.utimf.com
- www.crisil.com
- www.mutualfundsindia.com
- www.nseindia.com
- www.bseindia.com
- www.economictimes.indiatimes.com
- www.livemint.com
- www.finmin.nic.in
- www.businesstoday.intoday.in
- www.myiris.com
- www.indianotes.com
- www.money.rediff.com

Appendix – II

Insurance Companies in India | Mutual Funds in India |Broking Houses in India

INSURANCE SECTOR

General Insurance -

There are 4 Public Sector General Insurance Companies and 21 Private Sector General Insurance Companies

Public Sector General Insurance Companies –

National Insurance Co Ltd
New India Assurance Co Ltd
Oriental Insurance Co Ltd
United India Insurance Co Ltd

Private Sector General Insurance Companies

Acko General Insurance Co. Ltd.
Bajaj Allianz Allianz General Insurance Co. Ltd
Bharti AXA General Insurance Co. Ltd.
Cholamandalam MS General Insurance Co. Ltd.
DHFL General Insurance Co. Ltd
Edelweiss General Insurance Co. Ltd.
Future Generali India Insurance Co. Ltd.
Go Digit General Insurance Co. Ltd
HDFC ERGO General Insurance Co.Ltd.
ICICI LOMBARD General Insurance Co. Ltd.
IFFCO TOKIO General Insurance Co. Ltd.
Kotak Mahindra General Insurance Co. Ltd.
Liberty General Insurance Co. Ltd.
Magma HDI General Insurance Co. Ltd.
Raheja QBE General Insurance Co. Ltd.
Reliance General Insurance Co.Ltd
Royal Sundaram General Insurance Co. Ltd.
SBI General Insurance Co. Ltd.

Shriram General Insurance Co. Ltd.
Tata AIG General Insurance Company Ltd.
Universal Sompo General Insurance Co. Ltd.

Life Insurance Companies

In life insurance there are 24 companies out of which 23 are private life insurance companies

Public Sector Life Insurance Companies

Life Insurance Corporation of India

Private Sector Life Insurance Companies

Aditya Birla SunLife Insurance Co. Ltd.
Aegon Life Insurance Company Ltd.,
Aviva Life Insurance Company India Ltd.
Bajaj Allianz Life Insurance Co. Ltd.
Bharti AXA Life Insurance Company Ltd,
Canara HSBC Oriental Bank of Commerce Life Insurance Company Ltd.
DHFL Pramerica Life Insurance Co. Ltd.
Edelweiss Tokio Life Insurance Company Ltd.,3rd & 4th Floor,
Exide Life Insurance Co. Ltd.
Future Generali India Life Insurance Company Ltd.
HDFC Standard Life Insurance Co. Ltd
ICICI Prudential Life Insurance Co. Ltd,
IDBI Federal Life Insurance Company Ltd.
IndiaFirst Life Insurance Company Ltd.,
Kotak Mahindra Life Insurance Co. Ltd.
Max Life Insurance Co. Ltd.
PNB MetLife India Insurance Co. Ltd,
Reliance Nippon Life Insurance Company Ltd.,
Sahara India Life Insurance Co. Ltd.
SBI Life Insurance Co. Ltd.
Shriram Life Insurance Co. Ltd.
Star Union Dai-Ichi Life Insurance Co. Ltd.
TATA AIA Life Insurance Co. Ltd.

Standalone Health Insurance Companies
Aditya Birla Health Insurance Co. Ltd.
Apollo Munich Health Insurance Co. Ltd
CIGNA TTK Health Insurance Co. Ltd.
Max Bupa Health Insurance Co. Ltd
Star Health & Allied Insurance Co.Ltd.
Reliance Health Insurance Ltd.
Religare Health Insurance Co. Ltd

Export Credit Guarantee Insurance Companies
Export Credit Guarantee Corporation of India

Agriculture Insurance Companies
Agriculture insurance co. of India Ltd.

Re-insurance Companies
General Insurance Corporation of India - Re-Insuer

AMCs (Mutual Funds)
In India we have following Mutual Fund Companies. Securities Exchange Board of India (SEBI) is the regulatory body for all the mutual funds mentioned above. All the mutual funds must get registered with SEBI. The only exception is the UTI, since it is a corporation formed under a separate Act of Parliament.

Aditya Birla Sun Life AMC Ltd.
Axis Asset Management Company Ltd.
Baroda Pioneer Asset Management Company Ltd.
BNP Paribas Asset Management India Private Ltd.
BOI AXA Investment Managers Private Ltd.
Canara Robeco Asset Management Company Ltd.
DHFL Pramerica Asset Managers Private Ltd.
DSP Investment Managers Private Ltd.
Edelweiss Asset Management Ltd.
Essel Finance AMC Ltd.
Franklin Templeton Asset Management (India) Private Ltd.
HDFC Asset Management Company Ltd.

HSBC Asset Management (India) Private Ltd.
ICICI Prudential Asset Management Company Ltd.
IDBI Asset Management Ltd.
IDFC Asset Management Company Ltd.
IIFCL Asset Management Co. Ltd.
IIFL Asset Management Ltd.
IL&FS Infra Asset Management Ltd.
Indiabulls Asset Management Company Ltd.
Invesco Asset Management (India) Private Ltd.
ITI Asset Management Ltd.
JM Financial Asset Management Ltd.
Kotak Mahindra Asset Management Company Ltd.
L&T Investment Management Ltd.
LIC Mutual Fund Asset Management Ltd.
Mahindra Asset Management Company Pvt. Ltd.
Mirae Asset Global Investments (India) Pvt. Ltd.
Motilal Oswal Asset Management Company Ltd.
PPFAS Asset Management Pvt. Ltd.
Principal Asset Management Pvt. Ltd.
Quant Money Managers Ltd.
Quantum Asset Management Company Private Ltd.
Reliance Nippon Life Asset Management Ltd.
Sahara Asset Management Company Private Ltd.
SBI Funds Management Private Ltd.
Shriram Asset Management Co. Ltd.
SREI Mutual Fund Asset Management Pvt. Ltd.
Sundaram Asset Management Company Ltd.
Tata Asset Management Ltd.
Taurus Asset Management Company Ltd.
Union Asset Management Company Private Ltd.
UTI Asset Management Company Ltd
Yes Asset Management

BROKING HOUSES IN INDIA

The stock market is an important part of the economy of a country. The stock market plays a pivotal role in the growth of the industry and commerce of the country that eventually affects the economy of the country to a great extent. For this reason, the government, industry and even the central banks of the country keep a close watch on the happenings of the stock market. The stock market is important from both the industry's point of view as well as the investor's point of view.

A stockbroker is a regulated professional individual, usually associated with a brokerage firm or broker-dealer, who buys and sells shares and other securities for both retail and institutional clients, through a stock exchange or over the counter, in return for a fee or commission. Stockbrokers are known by numerous professional designations, depending on the license they hold, the type of securities they sell, or the services they provide. In most English speaking venues, the two-word term stock broker, like stock brokerage, normally applies to the brokerage firm, rather than to the individual.

Following is a partial list of the broking houses in India:

- KOTAK SECURITIES LTD
- SHAREKHAN LTD
- ANGEL BROKING LTD
- INDIA INFOLINE LTD
- RELIANCE MONEY
- INDIA BULLS
- ICICI DIRECT
- MOTILAL OSWAL SECURITIES
- GEOJIT BNP PARIBAS
- KARVY STOCK BROKING
- RELIGARE
- SMC GLOBAL SECURITES
- BONANZA ONLINE
- HDFC SECURITIES
- ANANDRATHI SECURITIES

Appendix – III

Tax Rates FY 2018 - 19 & FY 19-20*
Individuals and HUFs

I. Individual (other than II and III below) and HUF

	Income Level / Slabs	Income Tax Rate
i.	Up to ₹. 2,50,000	NIL
ii.	Income above ₹. 2,50,000 and up to ₹. 5,00,000	5% of the amount above total income of ₹. 2,50,000 Less: Tax Credit u/s 87A - " ₹. 2,500 for a taxable income upto ₹. 3.5 lac"
iii.	Income above ₹. 5,00,000 and up to ₹. 10,00,000	₹. 12,500+ 20% of the amount above total income of ₹. 5,00,000
iv.	Income above ₹. 10,00,000	₹. 1,12,500 + 30% of the amount above total income of ₹. 10,00,000

II. An individual resident who is of the age of 60 years or more but below the age of 80 years at any time during the previous year

	Income Level / Slabs	Income Tax Rate
i.	Up to ₹. 3,00,000.	NIL
ii.	Income above ₹. 3,00,000 and up to ₹. 5,00,000	5% of the amount above total income of ₹. 3,00,000 Less: Tax Credit u/s 87A - ₹. 2500 for a taxable income upto ₹. 3.5 lac
iii.	Income above ₹. 5,00,000 and up to ₹. 10,00,000	₹. 10,000 + 20% of the amount above total income of ₹. 5,00,000
iv.	Income above ₹. 10,00,000	₹. 110,000 + 30% of the amount above total income of ₹. 10,00,000.

III. An individual resident who is of the age of 80 years or more at any time during the previous year

	Income Level / Slabs	Income Tax Rate
i.	Up to ₹. 5,00,000	NIL

ii.	Income above ₹. 5,00,000 and up to ₹. 10,00,000	20% of the amount above total income of ₹. 5,00,000
iii.	Income above ₹. 10,00,000	₹. 100,000/- + 30% of the amount above total income of ₹. 10,00,000.

Surcharge: 10% on the total income tax for individuals earning between ₹ 50 lakh and ₹ 1 crore, 15% for those with income above ₹ 1 crore

Education Cess : 4% of the income tax and surcharge

Summary of Deductions

* For FY 19-20 in the interim budget Tax Credit u/s 87A - ₹ 12500 for a taxable income upto ₹ 5 lac

Deduction under section 80C: ₹ 150,000; Deduction under section 80CCD (NPS): ₹ 50,000; Interest for self-occupied property: ₹ 200,000; Deduction under section 80D: ₹ 25,000;

Section	Tax Exemption Limit	Eligible Investments
24B	**₹ 2 lac**	Payment of interest on Home Loan
80C	**₹ 1.5 lac**	• 15 years PPF (Public Provident Fund) • Contribution to EPF (Employees' Provident Fund) • Five years bank or post office tax saving deposits • NSC (National Savings Certificates) • SCSS (Post office Senior Citizen Savings Scheme) • ELSS (Equity Linked Savings Schemes) of mutual funds • Children's Tuition Fees • Principal repayment of home loan • NPS (National Pension System) of PFRDA • Life Insurance Premium *Sukanya Samriddhi Account Deposit Scheme* (newly introduced)
80CCC	**₹ 1.5 lac**	Contribution to annuity plan of life insurance company
80CCD	**₹ 50,000**	Notified Pension Schemes
80D	**₹ 25,000**	Health insurance premium (For senior citizen the limit is ₹ 50000)
80E	-	Interest payment of an education loan

Standard deduction increased from ₹ 40,000 (FY 18-19) to ₹ 50,000 (FY 19-20)

Appendix – IV

About Stock & Commodities exchanges

Stock Exchanges - India has a vibrant stock market, following are the key stock exchanges:

BSE Ltd
India International Exchange (India INX)
Metropolitan Stock Exchange of India Ltd
National Stock Exchange of India Ltd. (NSE)
NSE IFSC Ltd

Commodity Exchanges : India has a dynamic commodities market. In addition to regional commodities market following are the key Commodity Derivatives Exchanges:

- Ace Derivatives and Commodity Exchange Ltd.
- Indian Commodity Exchange Ltd.
- Multi Commodity Exchange of India Ltd.
- National Commodity & Derivatives Exchange Ltd.
- National Multi Commodity Exchange of India Ltd..

Recently BSE and NSE also have launched trading in commodities derivatives.

Appendix – V

Financial Knowledge Resources

Selected Commonly Viewed Business News Channels:

Cnbc tv18
Ndtv profit
Zee business
Cnbc awaz
Utv bloomberg
Et now

Selected Widely Circulated Business/Financial Dailies:

Economic times
Business standard
Mint
Dna money
Financial express
The hindu business line
Financial chronicle

Selected Business/Financial Magazines:

Business Today
Forbes India
India Business
Outlook Business
Outlook Money
Money Today
Business Week

Appendix - VII

Regulatory Authorities

Reserve Bank of India (RBI): Reserve Bank of India is the apex monetary institution of India. It is also called the central bank of the country. Though originally privately owned, since nationalisation in 1949, the Reserve Bank is fully owned by the Government of India. It acts as the apex monetary authority of the country. www.rbi.org.in

Securities and Exchange Board of India (SEBI): SEBI Act, 1992: The Securities and Exchange Board of India (SEBI) was established in the year 1988 as a non-statutory body for regulating the securities market. It became an autonomous body in 1992 and more powers were given through an ordinance. Since then it regulates the market through its independent powers. www.sebi.gov.in

Insurance Regulatory and Development Authority (IRDA): The Insurance Regulatory and Development Authority (IRDA) is a national agency of the Government of India and is based in Hyderabad (Andhra Pradesh). It was formed by an Act of Indian Parliament known as IRDA Act 1999, which was amended in 2002 to incorporate some emerging requirements. The mission of IRDA as stated in the act is "to protect the interests of the policyholders, to regulate, promote and ensure orderly growth of the insurance industry and for matters connected therewith or incidental thereto." www.irda.gov.in

PFRDA - Under the Finance Ministry, Pension Fund Regulatory and Development Authority: PFRDA was established by the Government of India on 23rd August, 2003. The government has, through an executive order dated 10th October 2003, mandated PFRDA to act as a regulator for the pension sector. The mandate of PFRDA is development and regulation of pension sector in India. www.pfrda.org.in

Appendix – VIII

Financial Planning Easy Tables — Amount in ₹

Year	Inflation Table Table 1	Standard Table Table 2	Future Amount Table - Regular Investment Table 3	Future Amount Table - One time Investment Table 4	Present Amount Table - One time Investment Table 5
Description	How price would grow, item of 1000 would become	Amount needed today for 1000 per month for next --years	Regular investment of 1000 per month would become	One-time investment of 1000 would become	Amount needed today to get 1000 in -- years
1	1060	11,538	12,000	1,100	909
2	1124	22,633	25,200	1,210	826
3	1191	33,301	39,720	1,331	751
4	1262	43,559	55,692	1,464	683
5	1338	53,422	73,261	1,611	621
6	1419	62,906	92,587	1,772	564
7	1504	72,025	1,13,846	1,949	513
8	1594	80,793	1,37,231	2,144	467
9	1689	89,224	1,62,954	2,358	424
10	1791	97,331	1,91,249	2,594	386
11	1898	1,05,126	2,22,374	2,853	350
12	2012	1,12,621	2,56,611	3,138	319
13	2133	1,19,828	2,94,273	3,452	290
14	2261	1,26,757	3,35,700	3,797	263
15	2397	1,33,421	3,81,270	4,177	239
16	2540	1,39,828	4,31,397	4,595	218
17	2693	1,45,988	4,86,536	5,054	198
18	2854	1,51,912	5,47,190	5,560	180
19	3026	1,57,607	6,13,909	6,116	164
20	3207	1,63,084	6,87,300	6,727	149
21	3400	1,68,350	7,68,030	7,400	135
22	3604	1,73,413	8,56,833	8,140	123
23	3820	1,78,282	9,54,516	8,954	112
24	4049	1,82,964	10,61,968	9,850	102
25	4292	1,87,465	11,80,165	10,835	92
26	4549	1,91,793	13,10,181	11,918	84
27	4822	1,95,955	14,53,199	13,110	76
28	5112	1,99,957	16,10,519	14,421	69
29	5418	2,03,805	17,83,571	15,863	63
30	5743	2,07,504	19,73,928	17,449	57
31	6088	2,11,062	21,83,321	19,194	52
32	6453	2,14,483	24,13,653	21,114	47
33	6841	2,17,772	26,67,019	23,225	43

34	7251	2,20,934	29,45,720	25,548	39
35	7686	2,23,975	32,52,292	28,102	36
36	8147	2,26,899	35,89,522	30,913	32
37	8636	2,29,711	39,60,474	34,004	29
38	9154	2,32,414	43,68,521	37,404	27
39	9704	2,35,014	48,17,373	41,145	24
40	10286	2,37,513	53,11,111	45,259	22

Assuming average inflation @6% p.a.

Assuming return on investment @10% p.a.

How to use "Financial Planning Easy Tables"

Inflation Table, Table 1
How price would grow, item of ₹ 1,000 would become

Standard Table, Table 2
Amount needed today for ₹ 1.000 per month for next – Years

Future Amount Table – Regular Investment, Table 3
Regular investment of ₹ 1,000 per month would become

Future Amount Table – One-time Investment, Table 4
One time investment of ₹ 1,000 would become

Present Amount Table – One-time Investment, Table 5
Amount needed today to get ₹ 1,000 in – years

Appendix – IX

FVIFL Tables

Year	4%	5%	6%	7%	8%	9%	10%	12%	14%	16%	18%	20%
1	1.04	1.05	1.06	1.07	1.08	1.09	1.1	1.12	1.14	1.16	1.18	1.2
2	1.082	1.102	1.124	1.145	1.166	1.188	1.21	1.254	1.3	1.346	1.392	1.44
3	1.125	1.158	1.191	1.225	1.26	1.295	1.331	1.405	1.482	1.561	1.643	1.728
4	1.17	1.216	1.262	1.311	1.36	1.412	1.464	1.574	1.689	1.811	1.939	2.074
5	1.217	1.276	1.338	1.403	1.469	1.539	1.611	1.762	1.925	2.1	2.288	2.488
6	1.265	1.34	1.419	1.501	1.587	1.677	1.772	1.974	2.195	2.436	2.7	2.986
7	1.316	1.407	1.504	1.606	1.714	1.828	1.949	2.211	2.502	2.826	3.185	3.583
8	1.369	1.477	1.594	1.718	1.851	1.993	2.144	2.476	2.853	3.278	3.759	4.3
9	1.423	1.551	1.689	1.838	1.999	2.172	2.358	2.773	3.252	3.803	4.435	5.16
10	1.48	1.629	1.791	1.967	2.159	2.367	2.594	3.106	3.707	4.411	5.234	6.192
11	1.539	1.71	1.898	2.105	2.332	2.58	2.853	3.479	4.226	5.117	6.176	7.43
12	1.601	1.796	2.012	2.252	2.518	2.813	3.138	3.896	4.818	5.936	7.288	8.916
13	1.665	1.886	2.113	2.41	2.72	3.066	3.452	4.363	5.492	6.886	8.599	10.699
14	1.732	1.98	2.261	2.579	2.937	3.342	3.797	4.887	6.261	7.988	10.147	12.839
15	1.801	2.079	2.397	2.759	3.172	3.642	4.177	5.474	7.138	9.266	11.974	15.407
16	1.873	2.183	2.54	2.952	3.426	3.97	4.595	6.13	8.137	10.748	14.129	18.488
17	1.948	2.292	2.693	3.159	3.7	4.328	5.054	6.866	9.276	12.468	16.672	22.186
18	2.026	2.407	2.854	3.38	3.996	4.717	5.56	7.69	10.575	14.463	19.673	26.623
19	2.107	2.527	3.026	3.617	4.316	5.142	6.116	8.613	12.056	16.777	23.214	31.948
20	2.191	2.653	3.207	3.87	4.661	5.604	6.728	9.646	13.743	19.461	27.393	38.338
25	2.666	3.386	4.292	5.427	6.848	8.623	10.835	17	26.462	40.874	62.669	95.396
30	3.243	4.322	5.743	7.612	10.063	13.268	17.449	29.96	50.95	85.85	143.371	237.376

FVIFA Tables

Year	4%	5%	6%	7%	8%	9%	10%	12%	14%	16%	18%	20%
1	1	1	1	1	1	1	1	1	1	1	1	1
2	2.04	2.05	2.06	2.07	2.08	2.09	2.1	2.12	2.14	2.16	2.18	2.2
3	3.122	3.152	3.184	3.215	3.246	3.278	3.31	3.374	3.44	3.506	3.572	3.64
4	4.246	4.31	4.375	4.44	4.506	4.573	4.641	4.779	4.921	5.066	5.215	5.368
5	5.416	5.526	5.637	5.751	5.867	5.985	6.105	6.353	6.61	6.877	7.154	7.442
6	6.633	6.802	6.975	7.153	7.336	7.523	7.716	8.115	8.536	8.977	9.442	9.93
7	7.898	8.142	8.394	8.654	8.923	9.2	9.487	10.089	10.73	11.414	12.142	12.916
8	9.214	9.549	9.897	10.26	10.637	11.028	11.436	12.3	13.233	14.24	15.327	16.499
9	10.583	11.027	11.491	11.978	12.488	13.021	13.579	14.776	16.085	17.518	19.086	20.799
10	12.006	12.578	13.181	13.816	14.487	15.193	15.937	17.549	19.337	21.321	23.521	25.959
11	13.486	14.207	14.972	15.784	16.645	17.56	18.531	20.655	23.044	25.733	28.755	32.15
12	15.026	15.917	16.87	17.888	18.977	20.141	21.384	24.133	27.271	30.85	34.931	39.58
13	16.627	17.713	18.882	20.141	21.495	22.953	24.523	28.029	32.089	36.786	42.219	48.497
14	18.292	19.599	21.015	22.55	24.215	26.019	27.975	32.393	37.581	43.672	50.818	59.196
15	20.024	21.579	23.276	25.129	27.152	29.361	31.772	37.28	43.842	51.66	60.965	72.035
16	21.825	23.657	25.673	27.888	30.324	33.003	35.95	42.753	50.98	60.925	72.939	87.442
17	23.698	25.84	28.213	30.84	33.75	36.974	40.545	48.884	59.118	71.673	87.068	105.931
18	25.645	28.132	30.906	33.999	37.45	41.301	45.599	55.75	68.394	84.141	103.74	128.117
19	27.671	30.539	33.76	37.379	41.466	46.018	51.159	63.44	78.969	98.603	123.414	154.74
20	29.778	33.066	36.786	40.995	45.762	51.16	57.275	72.052	91.025	115.38	146.628	186.688
25	41.646	47.727	54.865	63.249	73.106	84.701	98.347	133.334	181.871	249.214	342.603	471.981
30	56.805	66.439	79.058	94.461	113.283	136.308	164.494	241.333	356.787	530.312	790.948	1181.882

PVIFL Table

Period	4%	5%	6%	7%	8%	9%	10%	12%	14%	16%	18%	20%
1	0.962	0.952	0.943	0.935	0.926	0.917	0.909	0.893	0.877	0.862	0.847	0.833
2	0.925	0.907	0.890	0.873	0.857	0.842	0.826	0.797	0.769	0.743	0.718	0.694
3	0.889	0.864	0.840	0.816	0.794	0.772	0.751	0.712	0.675	0.641	0.609	0.579
4	0.855	0.823	0.792	0.763	0.735	0.708	0.683	0.636	0.592	0.552	0.516	0.482
5	0.822	0.784	0.747	0.713	0.681	0.650	0.621	0.567	0.519	0.476	0.437	0.402
6	0.790	0.746	0.705	0.666	0.630	0.596	0.564	0.507	0.456	0.410	0.370	0.335
7	0.760	0.711	0.665	0.623	0.583	0.547	0.513	0.452	0.400	0.354	0.314	0.279
8	0.731	0.677	0.627	0.582	0.540	0.502	0.467	0.404	0.351	0.305	0.266	0.233
9	0.703	0.645	0.592	0.544	0.500	0.460	0.424	0.361	0.308	0.263	0.225	0.194
10	0.676	0.614	0.558	0.508	0.463	0.422	0.386	0.322	0.270	0.227	0.191	0.162
11	0.650	0.585	0.527	0.475	0.429	0.388	0.350	0.287	0.237	0.195	0.162	0.135
12	0.625	0.557	0.497	0.444	0.397	0.356	0.319	0.257	0.208	0.168	0.137	0.112
13	0.601	0.530	0.469	0.415	0.368	0.326	0.290	0.229	0.182	0.145	0.116	0.093
14	0.577	0.505	0.442	0.388	0.340	0.299	0.263	0.205	0.160	0.125	0.099	0.078
15	0.555	0.481	0.417	0.362	0.315	0.275	0.239	0.183	0.140	0.108	0.084	0.065
16	0.534	0.458	0.394	0.339	0.292	0.252	0.218	0.163	0.123	0.093	0.071	0.054
17	0.513	0.436	0.371	0.317	0.270	0.231	0.198	0.146	0.108	0.080	0.060	0.045
18	0.494	0.416	0.350	0.296	0.250	0.212	0.180	0.130	0.095	0.069	0.051	0.038
19	0.475	0.396	0.331	0.277	0.232	0.194	0.164	0.116	0.083	0.060	0.043	0.031
20	0.456	0.377	0.312	0.258	0.215	0.178	0.149	0.104	0.073	0.051	0.037	0.026
25	0.375	0.295	0.233	0.184	0.146	0.116	0.092	0.059	0.038	0.024	0.016	0.010
30	0.308	0.231	0.174	0.131	0.099	0.075	0.057	0.033	0.020	0.012	0.007	0.004

PVIFA Table

Period	4%	5%	6%	7%	8%	9%	10%	12%	14%	16%	18%	20%
1	0.962	0.952	0.943	0.935	0.926	0.917	0.909	0.893	0.877	0.862	0.847	0.833
2	1.886	1.859	1.833	1.808	1.783	1.759	1.736	1.690	1.647	1.605	1.566	1.528
3	2.775	2.723	2.673	2.624	2.577	2.531	2.487	2.402	2.322	2.246	2.174	2.106
4	3.630	3.546	3.465	3.387	3.312	3.240	3.170	3.037	2.914	2.798	2.690	2.589
5	4.452	4.329	4.212	4.100	3.993	3.890	3.791	3.605	3.433	3.274	3.127	2.991
6	5.242	5.076	4.917	4.767	4.623	4.486	4.355	4.111	3.889	3.685	3.498	3.326
7	6.002	5.786	5.582	5.389	5.206	5.033	4.868	4.564	4.288	4.039	3.812	3.605
8	6.733	6.463	6.210	5.971	5.747	5.535	5.335	4.968	4.639	4.344	4.078	3.837
9	7.435	7.108	6.802	6.515	6.247	5.995	5.759	5.328	4.946	4.607	4.303	4.031
10	8.111	7.722	7.360	7.024	6.710	6.418	6.145	5.650	5.216	4.833	4.494	4.192
11	8.760	8.306	7.887	7.499	7.139	6.805	6.495	5.938	5.453	5.029	4.656	4.327
12	9.385	8.863	8.384	7.943	7.536	7.161	6.814	6.194	5.660	5.197	4.793	4.439
13	9.986	9.394	8.853	8.358	7.904	7.487	7.103	6.424	5.842	5.342	4.910	4.533
14	10.563	9.899	9.295	8.745	8.244	7.786	7.367	6.628	6.002	5.468	5.008	4.611
15	11.118	10.380	9.712	9.108	8.559	8.061	7.606	6.811	6.142	5.575	5.092	4.675
16	11.652	10.838	10.106	9.447	8.851	8.313	7.824	6.974	6.265	5.668	5.162	4.730
17	12.166	11.274	10.477	9.763	9.122	8.544	8.022	7.120	6.373	5.749	5.222	4.775
18	12.659	11.690	10.828	10.059	9.372	8.756	8.201	7.250	6.467	5.818	5.273	4.812
19	13.134	12.085	11.158	10.336	9.604	8.950	8.365	7.366	6.550	5.877	5.316	4.843
20	13.590	12.462	11.470	10.594	9.818	9.129	8.514	7.469	6.623	5.929	5.353	4.870
25	15.622	14.094	12.783	11.654	10.675	9.823	9.077	7.843	6.873	6.097	5.467	4.948
30	17.292	15.372	13.765	12.409	11.258	10.274	9.427	8.055	7.003	6.177	5.517	4.979

References

Web Resources:
www.journalofpersonalfinance.com
pfp.missouri.edu
www.cfainstitute.org
www.aciia.org
www.fpsbindia.org
http://www.planandact.com
www.onefpa.org
www.amfiindia.com
www.fpa.com.au
www.investorprotection.org
www.valueresearchonline.com
http://www.prudential.com

Books:
Everyone's Guide to Financial Planning by Helen P. Rogers
Lessons on Financial Planning for Young Investors by SEBI
Ernst & Young's *Personal Financial Planning Guide, 5th Edition* by Martin Nissenbaum, Barbara J. Raasch, Charles L. Ratner. [John Wiley & Sons, Inc.]
Personal Finance for Dummies, 6th Edition by Eric Tyson, MBA [Wiley]

Financial Management Theory & Practice, 7th Edition by Prasanna Chandra Tata [McGraw-Hill]
Financial Advisor Series: FOUNDATIONS OF FINANCIAL PLANNING: AN OVERVIEW Allen McLellan (Editor) [The American College Press]

Articles:

10 golden rules of investing: How to secure your financial future by Riju Mehta [ET Bureau]
Life Cycle of Financial Planning [www.takechargetoday.arizona.edu]
Managing Household Records [www.usa.gov]
Quantifying the Economic Benefits of Personal Financial Planning by Sherman D. Hanna, Suzanne Lindamood [www.academyfinancial.org]

What experts say about the book

"Understanding the basics of Financial Planning is essential if one wants to design a prosperous future for his family. That's where "*The Money Mindset*" *book* comes in. Outlining key strategies on financial planning, the book is packed with interesting and yet thought-provoking content. Providing readers with need-to-know tips and tools to succeed, *The Money Mindset book* gives everything that one needs to know about this significant concept call- Personal Financial Planning. Vinay does an excellent job of translating his years of financial services experience into a book that can be enjoyed and understood by all. This is easily a good read for anyone who wants to create & maintain wealth. As part of one of the prominent global financial education institution, I strongly recommend this book to all those who would like to take control of their personal finance."

- **Aditya Gadge, Chief Executive Officer, Association of International Wealth Management of India**

"Vinay's book on Personal Finance gives a practitioner's view on Financial Planning and is a mandatory reading for all who find the world of investments very complex and confusing. Vinay uses his experience in presenting the complex art of financial planning in a lucid manner and demystifies the arcane world of investments to the layman. I am sure that Vinay's book would be useful to the many who are today unsure about planning for their financial goals"

- **Rajendra Kalur, CFA CFP^{CM}, Director & Chief Executive Officer , TrustPlutus Wealth Managers (India) Private Limited TM**

"Vinay has written an excellent teach-yourself finance primer for non-finance executives, and, I dare say, even for most finance executives. The simple lucid style enables effortless learning of key concepts, the understanding of which is greatly enhanced by relevant and practical examples from the real world. This is a must-read for all who are keen on planning their future. India is going to witness massive migration of capital from physical assets to financial assets over next few years and this book can be serve your purpose of creating long term wealth."

- **Manish Bhandari, CEO and Portfolio Manager Vallum Capital Advisors**

Dear Reader , Acquiring wealth is your right, gaining wealth is a virtue and where as scientific financial planning goes a long way in creating wealth. This book suggests a very practical and step-by-step approach to financial planning. I must congratulate the author for narrating a complicated subject in such an lucid way. Readers should make full use of the book to get the maximum personal benefit.

I am sure every reader will find this book interesting, helpful in planning their finances and building a robust financial plan to achieve their financial dreams. I congratulate Vinay for coming out with this book, which is essentially a tool for the readers to achieve financial security with certainty. The take away for me is that one needs to ' Dream more' , 'Plan for it' in writing and 'Implement the plan with Discipline' for achieving it.

- **Rajev B Sharma, Group MD & CEO - TASA Asia, Founder – Victory.Inc**

About the Author

Vinay Mahajan has keen interest and extensive experience in the Wealth Management and Investment Banking domain. He has over 20 years of professional experience as an Academician, Corporate Trainer, Financial Products Expert, Sales and Business Head. Academically he holds B.E., M.Tech, CFA (ICFAI) and CIIA (ACIIA, Germany). He is an alumni of IIM-Calcutta and Certified Financial Planner$^{CM.}$ He is a regular investor educator and conducts seminars & workshops across India. He has been featured on business news channels, web chats and writing blogs on topics related to financial planning and advised people on Financial Planning.

He can be contacted at info@authorvinaymahajan.com

Please visit www.authorvinaymahajan.com for more on financial planning.

Disclaimer: The contents of this book are for general discussion only and not to be construed as advice for any financial transactions or performance assurance of any investment. The author and the publisher are not responsible for any financial transactions undertaken by the reader. Financial advice varies considerably based on one's risk profile. Readers are advised to consult their financial advisor or use their own wisdom to make any financial decisions. Return assumptions have been taken for illustration purposes only and do not indicate return from a particular investment generally or specifically. Wherever needed calculations/numbers have been rounded off for easy understanding or simplicity and it may not reflect mathematical accuracy or correctness. Contents of the book may undergo changes with time, readers may please get updated information from any source of their choice.

www.ingramcontent.com/pod-product-compliance
Lightning Source LLC
Chambersburg PA
CBHW022036190326
41520CB00008B/594

* 9 7 8 9 3 8 8 9 3 0 3 9 0 *